Just Schools

Just Schools

A Whole School Approach to Restorative Justice

Belinda Hopkins

Foreword and Introduction by Guy Masters

Jessica Kingsley Publishers
London and Philadelphia

First published in the United Kingdom in 2004
by Jessica Kingsley Publishers
116 Pentonville Road
London N1 9JB, UK
and
400 Market Street, Suite 400
Philadelphia, PA 19106, USA

www.jkp.com

Copyright © Belinda Hopkins 2004
Copyright Foreword and Introduction © Guy Masters 2004

Library of Congress Cataloging in Publication Data
A CIP catalog record for this book is available from the Library of Congress

British Library Cataloguing in Publication Data
A CIP catalogue record for this book is available from the British Library

ISBN 978 1 84310 132 1

Printed and Bound in Great Britain by
Athenaeum Press, Gateshead, Tyne and Wear

Contents

Appendices

List of Figures

List of Tables

Acknowledgements

First, I would like to thank everyone with whom I have worked over the past ten years or so in the field of conflict management, circle time, alternatives to violence, mediation and restorative justice. I have tried to mention direct sources of inspiration, but over the years it becomes difficult to remember where all the different ideas have come from. I acknowledge that the ingredients here come from many sources, and my contribution is to have cooked them up into a new dish called 'Just Schools'.

I owe a huge debt of thanks to the international restorative justice community, many of whom have known that I have been writing this book, and have sent me ideas and encouraging e-mails. Some people have even been kind enough to read bits of the book as I have been struggling over them. I want to mention particularly Nancy Riestenberg and Annie Warner Roberts in the United States, and Marg Thorsborne, Marg Armstrong, Brenda Morrison, Di Margetts and Peta Blood in Australia. How wonderful to learn from, and be supported by, such a powerful, visionary group of women.

It is also important to mention the influence and encouragement of seminal thinkers and practitioners like Terry O'Connell, Howard Zehr, David Moore and John Braithwaite who have been generous with their time and ideas, either face to face or by e-mail.

Closer to home, I want to thank those people I think of as my restorative justice family, the people who have encouraged me and given me so many opportunities to try out my ideas and develop my thinking – Charles Pollard, Debbie Hewer, Tony and Kathryn Walker, Maggie Kelly, Nic Brennan, Nicky Preston, Mel Lofty, Jackie Keyser, Sue Raikes, Patsy Townsend, Chris Harman, Richard Newcombe, Gordon Richardson, Graham Waddington, Hilary Cremin, Eemonn Keenan and, recently, Gary Fletcher and Mandy Watkins.

I want to thank Edmund Burke, Tom Heydeman and Hilary Reed, who took the time to read chapters and discuss them with me. I also want to thank the many friends who listened to me and picked me up when my confidence faltered, helping me to believe in myself and in the book – Nic Bayley, Amanda James, Morag (Miffy) Scally, Kirsty Dabbs, Fiona Elwell, John Mulligan, Dave Hamilton, Chris Kiely, Tim Carroll and Peter Burton. Many more friends have simply helped me by being there, and reminding me there is more to life than restorative justice (I humour them!). They are too many to mention, and I almost surely would miss someone out. I can only say how lucky I am to know them all.

I want to mention two very special people without whom this book would never have even been started – Guy Masters, whose wonderful Foreword and Introduction help to set this book in context, and Jerry Tyrrell.

Originally Guy, Jerry and I were going to write the book together. When Jerry became ill, Guy and I knew that we had to get on with it so that Jerry could at least contribute. Unfortunately Jerry died before he was able to do this, but his inspiration and his enthusiasm for restorative approaches in schools helped me enormously to develop my thinking on the subject, and I suspect he has been supporting me from somewhere. Subsequently Guy encouraged me to go it alone, because he knew I had something very important to say and he wanted to give me the chance to say it. I am very grateful for his generosity of spirit. His own wisdom, and his experience and knowledge of the wider field, shines through in the Introduction, and I think the book is richer for it.

Marian Liebmann deserves a special mention too, because she read the whole of the first draft of this book. Her incisive, brave and honest feedback helped me to see that the whole book needed rewriting. I hope she will think this version is an improvement. Marian has been a source of inspiration to me ever since I first began to think about how conflict management and mediation could transform schools. Furthermore it was she who recommended me to Jessica Kingsley just at the point when I was thinking it was time to find a publisher for the book I wanted to write. I owe her a great deal.

Finally, I want to thank my wider family for all of their support. My parents and my brother Jon have been so helpful in reading many of the chapters and giving me valuable feedback. Jon helped me with some of the early graphics, and from these have developed so much of my thinking around the various restorative processes. My brother Lindsay has inspired me with his own inner drive and positive approach, and this has helped when I have lost sight of the goal.

Not only do I want to thank my two beautiful and wonderful daughters, Bryony and Molly, for their patience, their encouragement, their belief in me and their love, I also want to thank them for the hard time they give me when I forget to 'walk the talk'. They have endured, all their lives, the new techniques, the new strategies and the occasionally poorly understood theories I have learned about and tried out on them.

'Call yourself a conflict management trainer?' they cry, when it all goes wrong! And hurray for that – or else I would never learn what works and what doesn't…so thank you!

My last big thank you is for the one person without whom not only would this book not have been written, but also nor would I have even dared to embark on the work in the first place. His unstinting support and encouragement, his practical help when my computing skills let me down, his patient reading of every chapter as it emerged from the printer, his patience and his sensitive feedback, all this leaves me almost speechless with gratitude. So my last thank you is to someone who has walked the talk all his life, and has taught me that 'love' is a verb, and not just a feeling. Thank you, Michael.

Special note

With the exception of Chapter 2, all chapters are preceded by a quotation from participants on one of the first courses designed specifically with the needs of school-based personnel in mind. I invited them to say what restorative justice meant to them at the end of the six-week course.

Foreword

I believe that this book could soon become a critically important restorative justice text, and deservedly so. It should prove valuable to both newcomers to restorative practice, and to experienced practitioners. There are many excellent books about restorative justice available; however, the key focus of this book is entirely different – it is a book about the values, and skills, that underpin all restorative practice. Furthermore, this book explores how individuals within communities can transform their daily interactions for the positive, so that all can feel more valued, as well as how they deal with the inevitable conflicts that will occur. Belinda has chosen to demonstrate how this transformation can be achieved within a school community, but the principles and techniques described are equally applicable to other organisations. The true importance of this book is that it sets down, in a readily accessible style and format, how any community can begin to change how they interact with one another, and deal with conflict in a socially inclusive manner.

This book has been written close to 25 years after the first restorative justice projects were pioneered in criminal justice. Since these first projects were developed in the mid to late 1970s in Canada and North America, the range and breadth of restorative justice practice has grown significantly. These projects were attempting to introduce an entirely different way of working within the criminal justice system. The methods developed valued empowerment, communication and repair. It quickly became recognised that many victims need to be listened to and to have their say (often to the person responsible for the harm done), and that many offenders, given the opportunity, were willing to meet the people harmed by their actions, to talk through the impact of their actions and accept responsibility to do something to put things right as best they could. Rather than offenders being passive recipients of sentencing outcomes, and victims sidelined to appearing as trial witnesses (if needed), restorative approaches (such as victim–offender mediation and family group conferencing) recognise that these parties should be central to the process.

There are now many different forms of restorative practice in use, in over 70 countries (Umbreit 2001). This growth is no longer entirely driven by practitioners wanting to do things differently, but by governments who appear to have recognised what restorative justice has to offer. In England and Wales, for example, there is now both a legislative basis for undertaking restorative practice within the youth justice system, and government expectations that this will occur. I think that there are several clear reasons for this recent upsurge of interest in restorative practice. First, restorative practice has been very extensively evaluated in a wide variety of countries, and all evaluations are broadly positive. There is emerging evidence that, when practice is to a high standard, there is a reduction in re-offending rates (Miers *et al.* 2001). However, restorative practice has also been shown to often produce a wide range of other equally important benefits. Both offenders and victims, though they report that participation can be difficult, commonly report that they felt treated respectfully, and fairly. Critical amongst these is that the majority of victims who are involved in restorative practice report that it helped them put the offence and events behind them, often drastically reducing fears of further victimisation (Umbreit and Roberts 1996). I believe that a further reason for the upsurge of interest in restorative justice is that most talk about criminal justice and offending is profoundly negative, while restorative practice very often results in very positive outcomes in many cases of healing and forgiveness taking place, and new bonds being forged.

Guy Masters
Wandsworth Youth Offending Team

Preface

This is a book for everyone wanting to work in a school where people care about each other, and where good relationships, mutual respect and a sense of belonging are seen as key to successful teaching and learning. It is a book designed to inspire, enthuse and enable people with energy and commitment to create a school community in which, when harmful behaviour or conflicts occur, the emphasis is on repairing the damage caused to relationships and on finding mutually acceptable ways forward. This emphasis has the potential to transform the way that members of that school community think, feel and behave towards each other.

This is also a book for those who work inside or outside schools with young people who feel let down by their current educational experience. Such education professionals may feel they need a different approach. The young people they work with may be seeking to get their needs met in ways that impact negatively on others and may already be engaging in anti-social and illegal behaviour. These young people are in the care of adults who are trying very hard to understand their situation and are offering them support. This book offers such adults new ways to look at old challenges.

Although this book was written with the needs of teachers in mind, there is an increasing interest in developing restorative processes in schools from many other agencies who work with school-aged young people. Many of you may be opening this book for information about a particular restorative process or intervention. It is not for me to instruct you to read the whole book, although I would encourage you to do so, since the essential message of the book is that a 'Just School' integrates restorative principles and practice into every policy, every lesson, every meeting and every event in the school day.

Guy Masters' Introduction sets the subject of this book in the wider context of restorative justice nationally and internationally, in the early part of this new millennium. This Introduction attests to his deep understanding of the current relevance of restorative practices to the lives of victims and offenders, their friends, families and neighbours, and indeed to our society alike. He sets the scene for this book, and I am very grateful for that.

The use of the term 'restorative justice' in the school context is controversial, and practitioners in different parts of the world use different phrases. Some people do not agree that the word 'justice' is appropriate in the school context because of its links to the criminal justice field. 'Restorative practices' and 'restorative measures' are two alternative phrases used. Other people argue that the word 'restorative' is a misnomer because of the need to build as well as to restore relationships in a school community. However, the central inspirations behind the approach remain the same whatever phrase is used. Long after the term 'restorative justice' ceases to be 'flavour of the month' the ideas and approaches in this book will be valid. They have a long pedigree, and I can see a logical sequence in the development of the concepts, culminating in the terms and approaches articulated here.

I have divided the main book into three parts. Part I explains what is special about restorative justice, and describes how one might encourage and persuade others to consider introducing restorative principles and practices into their school. Part II explores restorative skills and practices and how to develop and use them, beginning with what is at the heart of all good restorative practice – active, empathic, non-judgemental, non-directive listening. From this essential base, the skills for de-escalating conflict when faced with challenging conversations oneself are explained. These skills are then further developed in the context of mediating others' conflicts and also when repairing the harm caused by inappropriate or anti-social behaviour. Part III suggests how to implement a whole school approach along restorative lines; it considers how to ensure that a restorative approach, once introduced, can be nurtured and sustained long after the first generation of enthusiasts have moved on.

There are many community building and community repair initiatives being adopted in schools where people have never heard of the term 'restorative justice'. Nevertheless, it is within this particular conceptual framework that many apparently disparate initiatives are brought together, perhaps for the first time, as a 'Whole School Approach'.

Introduction to Restorative Justice Ideas and Practice

The main focus of this book is the application of restorative practice in schools, though it is as relevant to criminal justice practitioners. This Introduction is intended to provide readers who are new to the restorative justice field with a brief overview of the historical development of restorative practice and restorative justice theory, including recent restorative justice developments within youth justice in England and Wales. This account of the wide range of restorative justice initiatives under way will, it is hoped, provide readers with the confidence to press forward in developing their own practice, based on the practical skills covered in the remainder of this book.

However, this book is set in a wider context – it has been written following a great deal of experience with restorative practice in many countries, and many settings. The evidence validates that restorative approaches do work very well, even in extreme cases. Mark Yantzi's (1998) pioneering work in the field of sexual offending and restoration is strong testimony to this, as is the experience in the United States of restorative justice in murder cases (Umbreit 2002), and New Zealand's experience of family group conferencing with serious and persistent offenders (Levine *et al.* undated). Consequently, after 25 years of experience, practitioners and policy makers should not be asking the question 'Does this work?' but 'How do we make this work here?' The unique contribution of this book to the field is that it describes precisely how to go about implementing a range of restorative practices to a high standard, without underestimating the difficulties that are often faced.

First developments in practice

The first documented attempt to introduce restorative practice into a criminal justice system was in Canada in 1975 (Wright 1996). Two young adults were due to be sentenced for vandalising 22 properties in their neighbourhood. The probation officer in this case was a member of a local Mennonite group that had been discussing how a Christian response to offending could be introduced into the criminal justice system (Peachey 1989). In this case of vandalism, the probation officer proposed that rather than impose a fine and probation, the judge make it a condition of their probation order that the two men meet with all of their victims to discuss repairing the damage, or compensating them for any costs. This was done very successfully and led to the same Mennonite planning a project to attempt to do this work on a systematic basis. In 1975 the first Victim–Offender Reconciliation Project (VORP) began in Ontario. The key objective of this project, as the name suggests, was to achieve 'reconciliation' between victims and offenders. This was to be done through offering victims and offenders the opportunity to communicate with each other through a mediator. Mediators were usually trained volunteers from the local community, or probation officers. The experience of this project quickly demonstrated the feasibility of victims and offenders communicating with one another about an offence, and discussing what offenders could do to make up for the harm they had caused, financially, or through material work. This experience greatly challenged assumptions that it was impossible for victims and offenders to discuss, between them, respectfully and safely, the offence that had occurred. However, while a key aim of the project was to achieve 'reconciliation' between victims and offenders, evaluation established that this was only important to a third of victims (Coates and Gehm 1989). Most victims valued being listened to, being able to ask questions, to explain how they had been affected, to ask for reparation, to see that the offender was remorseful and to see that the offender got some help. Offenders valued being listened to by their victims, and being able to negotiate how costs could be reimbursed. Very few victims or offenders were dissatisfied with their experience, though many found it difficult. Of all who participated, only one victim said that they would not enter mediation again (Coates and Gehm 1989).

As information about this project spread, similar projects began in the United States in the late 1970s, and in various European countries in the early 1980s, such as Austria, Germany and England. The results from many of the English projects, as with similar experiments in Europe and North America, were encouraging (Marshall and Merry 1990). Most victims and offenders welcomed the opportunity to be involved and many benefited greatly. For some victims, fear of further victimisation has been shown to halve (Umbreit and Roberts 1996), and the desire for revenge is also greatly diminished (Strang 2000). For many, the opportunity of mediation provides an 'ending' to this episode in their life. The following case study demonstrates how this can operate in practice, and has been chosen because of the education link.

Case study

Chris Stewart was 13 when he assisted in the burglary of his old primary school. As it was his first offence the police decided to issue a caution (this case pre-dates the introduction of reprimands and final warnings). Aware that there were likely to be other issues resulting from this incident, a worker with the local restorative justice team, part of the area's Youth Justice Services, went to see Chris and his family.

The visit revealed that Chris's mother had been particularly affected by the offence, and was feeling particularly ashamed because the headmaster of the school had done a lot to help Chris when he was a pupil there. Also the school was only two streets away, on the main road into the local town. She was now avoiding the road for fear of being seen by the headmaster or some of the other teachers. She expressed a strong interest in some meeting with the headmaster.

A subsequent visit to the headmaster, Mr Chapman, uncovered that the burglary was only the latest offence against the school, and that the school was being regularly vandalised. The staff were feeling particularly victimised because many of their ex-pupils would hang around near the school in the evenings, and the staff thought that the attacks were personal. The headmaster said he would be interested in a meeting with Chris and his mother.

A meeting was set for the following week, to take place in a local community hall during the evening. The day before the meeting, one of the team went to visit Chris and spent a few minutes alone with him to verify that he had thought about what he was going to say to the headmaster. Chris said that he knew it was going to be hard, but that he thought he should do it.

The meeting began with ground rules being established, and then it was left to the participants to say what they wanted to say to each other.

Mr Chapman immediately began by saying that he had respect for Chris for being willing to meet with him and that it showed him in a very good light. They then talked about the offence and Chris's involvement in it. Mr Chapman stressed that he had felt very surprised and disappointed when he heard that Chris had been involved. He also talked about the disruption to the school as the classroom had been closed for two days. He also talked about the anger and concern of the staff about the vandalism, and that it was being taken personally. Chris apologised for the disruption to the school.

Mrs Stewart talked about her deep feeling of shame, and that she was now concerned to walk past the school. Mr Chapman assured Mrs

Stewart that she should not feel like this, and that the school were not blaming her in any way, and that she was welcome to come and visit the school whenever she wished.

Prior to the meeting all the participants had been asked to think of what could be done to make up for what had happened. Mr Chapman said that he would appreciate it if the litter was cleared from the field next to the school, but he would really like Chris to talk to the other boys about how the school was being affected by the vandalism. Chris said that he would rather not clear the field as his friends would laugh at him, but that he would like to help out with the after-school football sessions, and that he would say something to his friends about the vandalism. After some discussion between all three participants, it was agreed that Mrs Stewart and Chris would clear the litter together one evening, and that Chris could help at football practice if he wanted to.

Follow-up phone calls by the team revealed that all participants were satisfied with how the case had been handled and with the outcome. Mr Chapman reported that the litter had been cleared and that Chris was still helping out with football every week voluntarily. However, the most beneficial outcome highlighted by the school was that they had not been vandalised since the meeting took place, which they attributed to Chris talking to his friends.

(courtesy of Chris Stevens)

However, there are also examples of poor practice, which have been highly publicised (Davis 1992). The most damning of these was that victims were being used to affect the sentence of offenders. In England at that time mediation was offered in cases where the mediation service, commonly run by the probation service (Marshall and Merry 1990), wished either to keep the offender from being prosecuted or to reduce their likely sentence (Davis 1992). Mediation was not being offered in *all* cases, or in those cases in which victims or offenders were likely to benefit from the actual process of mediation. This is an important point to note, as it illustrates how mediation can be abused and used discriminatorily. Consequently, the potential benefits offered to victims and offenders by restorative justice can be summarised as follows:

For victims

- To be given information about what is happening in their case.

- Having someone listen sympathetically to their experience (the mediator).

- The opportunity to have questions answered about why the offence occurred (answering 'why me?').

- The opportunity to tell the offender(s) how they had been affected.

- The opportunity to ask the offender for compensation or reparation of some sort.

- The opportunity to receive an apology, and see that the offender is genuinely remorseful.

- The opportunity to help the offender.

- The opportunity to meet them in a situation in which they are not powerless.

For offenders

- To acknowledge responsibility and fully face up to what they had done by hearing and acknowledging the harm caused to the victims.

- To show themselves in a better light by answering questions, apologising, and doing things to make amends for the harm.

For both victims and offenders

- The opportunity to be involved in making decisions about their case.

Further developments in practice

The second major model of practice to develop was 'family group conferencing' in New Zealand, which in 1990 (following legislation in 1989) was ambitiously used to reform their youth justice system (Maxwell and Morris 1993). There were at least three motivations for this reform. First, there was a strong motivation to greatly reduce the number of young people, particularly from the Maori population, entering the formal criminal justice system, and the numbers being sentenced to custody. Second, there had been significant criticism from the Maori about the existing Western European criminal justice system. These criticisms attacked the existing system for dealing with offenders as individuals in isolation from their families and communities. The Maori saw an offence as a sign of failure for a family, and the wider community, not just of the individual offender, and they wanted much greater involvement in the decision-making process. Third, and an extension of the previous concern, was that the victims of youth crime were ignored by the criminal justice process.

Following the 1989 Children, Young Persons, and Their Families Act in New Zealand, a principle was set that only the most serious and persistent young offenders would be prosecuted (Maxwell and Morris 1993). All decisions on how offenders should be treated would be guided by the following principles:

- criminal proceedings not to be instigated if there is an alternative means of dealing with the matter

- any measures taken should strengthen the young person and their family group

- the ability of family groups to deal with offending by their children should be fostered

- young people to be kept in the community while consonant with the need to ensure public safety

- age to be a mitigating factor in determining whether to impose sanctions, and the nature of any sanctions

- any sanctions to promote the development of the young person, and to take the least restrictive form

- due regard to be given to the interests of any victims.

In practice this means that 80 per cent of young offenders in New Zealand are dealt with through a police caution, which cannot be cited in court. This might involve the young person in some form of community activity, mediation with the victim, or paying some compensation. Half of the remaining 20 per cent are still not prosecuted, but are referred for a diversionary family group conference. Family group conferences are the second widespread form of restorative practice to be developed. The young offender will attend the FGC, accompanied by their immediate and extended family network, plus other 'supporters', such as friends and other adults that are significant to them. The victims of their offences will also be invited and can also attend with supporters. Also attending will be professionals who can advise the conference about programmes available to help the offender, such as drugs or alcohol counselling, or help with education. This group will meet together to:

- discuss the offence, enable the victims to ask questions of the offender, and say what they wish to say in a safe environment

- discuss the causes of the offending behaviour and how this can best be addressed.

A key aspect of family group conferencing is that the majority of the decision-making power rests with the young person, their family, and the victims. The professional workers are there as advisers, not decision makers. Following the discussions between the victim and the offender, and the information given by the professionals, the young person and their family are left *alone* to produce a plan that addresses the concerns of the victim, and the causes of the offending. In the FGC cases that are used to divert young people from prosecution, if the plan is acceptable to the police, then the young person will not be prosecuted, and is given a further warning. For the 10 per cent that are prosecuted, once they have been found guilty or admitted guilt, the court *cannot* pass sentence until an FGC has taken place. In New Zealand about 5000 FGCs are held annually. The plan created at the FGC is then considered at court when they sentence, and courts can only ignore the family plan if they believe that the community will be at risk from the young person. The only exceptions to the FGC procedures are young people who are charged with murder or manslaughter. In New Zealand FGC plans are created at 95 per cent of conferences, and these are accepted by courts, unchanged, 80 per cent of the time. Victims attend 50 per cent of conferences, with 60 per cent of victims who attend saying that they benefit from participation (Maxwell and Morris 1993). The overriding message from New Zealand is that the young people and families in the most challenging of circumstances do produce plans that impress the court when given the opportunity. The experience of other countries that have since implemented FGCs in some way matches the success of New Zealand (Jackson 1998; Marsh and Crow 1998).

Case study

Harry Stephenson (not his real name), a 16-year-old with 50 or 60 offences behind him, was saved from imminent custody and given a new outlook with a pre-sentence plan which followed a family group conference. Following his experience, Stephenson has urged another offender to enter the programme, writing that at his own conference 'all I saw was a group of the loveliest people I've ever known all doing their utmost to keep me out of prison'.

In a 90-day support plan, devised primarily by Stephenson and his family in a private session during the conference, he had mandatory meetings with the co-ordinator, a police officer and a Victim Support worker (who supervised a letter of apology) and regular supervision from a young offenders team social worker. He did community work at the police station, was introduced to new leisure activities and given a job by his uncle. That was a year ago, and he has since committed only one offence.

'The conference made me see things in a different perspective. I hadn't thought about the victim before. I just thought: "They've got it and I haven't." And I used to hate the police. Every time I passed them, I shouted abuse. But when I got to know them, I realised they are just doing their jobs. It was quite a surprise to hear how my family felt and thought, too.'

Stephenson's mother, Jan Barry (not her real name), says the conference was 'a turning point for the whole family'. 'It did a lot of good. For so long we'd been battling on our own against the tide, but after that, we had so many people to turn to. The thought of going there frightened me, and I think it frightened Harry, but instead of pointing the finger at him, everybody was saying: "What can we do to make things better?"'

(Mapp 1997, p.25)

Restorative conferencing

A third practice model to develop is now commonly referred to as 'restorative conferencing' within England and Wales. This model originated in New South Wales, Australia, where it was introduced in 1993 by police in the city of Wagga Wagga (Moore and Forsythe 1995). This model was inspired by the development of family group conferencing in New Zealand, but was also informed by criminological theory (Braithwaite 1989). This theory of 'reintegrative shaming' argued that offenders should be confronted with the full consequences of their actions, but in a situation of support and care that did not label them as offenders. Within restorative conferencing a neutral facilitator convenes a meeting attended by the offender and the victim(s), along with 'supporters' of both – commonly family and friends. This model also stresses the importance of having others attend who know the offender in a positive light, and can comment upon this. This model often follows a scripted format, in which questions intended to draw out the thoughts and feelings of all present are asked by the facilitator. As with mediation and FGCs, it is the group, not the facilitator, who decide what the offender might do to make amends for the offence, and how they might be assisted to remain out of further trouble. This model does not commonly use the private planning time endorsed with family group conferencing, stressing the importance of the entire group remaining together throughout the process. Much more is said about this model elsewhere in this book, and how it has been applied successfully in schools. As with mediation and FGCs, this model has also been positively evaluated in several countries (e.g. Hayes, Prenzler and Wortley 1998). In England and Wales it has been promoted by Thames Valley Police, Nottinghamshire Police and Surrey Police.

Recent developments in England and Wales

There have been two recent significant reforms of the youth justice system in England and Wales: the Crime and Disorder Act in 1998, and the Youth Justice and Criminal Evidence Act in 1999.

The 1998 Crime and Disorder Act is considered to be a very mixed piece of legislation. While it introduced great potential for the development of restorative practice, other aspects of the legislation have been greatly criticised for bringing far more young people who have committed very minor offences into the criminal justice system (Goldson 2000). This legislation introduced a strict system by which young people committing a first minor offence receive a reprimand (and are not prosecuted), and those who commit a second minor offence will then receive a final warning. Any further offence will result in their prosecution. Offenders committing a moderately serious first offence will probably progress immediately to a final warning with a second offence leading to prosecution. Any serious offence will see the young person prosecuted. All young people who receive final warnings or are prosecuted will come to the attention of youth offending teams (YOTs), also created nationally by the Crime and Disorder Act. YOTs comprise workers from five of the main agencies that work with young people: police, social workers, probation officers, health, and education. These are commonly supported by other specialists such as youth workers, drug or alcohol workers, or mental health specialists. The aim of this group is to be able to respond to any needs that young offenders may have in a co-ordinated style. YOTs are a sensible development with great potential.

The first point at which restorative practice is being applied within this system is at the reprimand/final warning stage. Home Office guidance strongly encourages the use of restorative practice as part of these diversionary measures, and the Youth Justice Board has invested significantly in providing training for all YOTs in the restorative conferencing model.

The Crime and Disorder Act did not explicitly legislate for any restorative justice process. What it did do, though, is introduce 'reparation' as a key aim for *all* young offenders, prosecuted or warned. There is a specific Reparation Order, and reparation is expected to play a key part of other orders that young people may be subjected to. Reparation is intended to be made either directly to the victims of the young person or to the community. YOTs are supposed to liaise with all victims of young people and offer them the opportunity to receive reparation from the young person, or recommend community work that they would like them to do. Reparation is intended to be of benefit to victims, and is a clear opportunity for the use of restorative processes, such as mediation (Mediation UK 2001). What has happened in practice is that some YOTs have seized this opportunity to develop mediation or family group conferencing, or both, while others have focused on engaging young people in community activities, and do not really look to involve victims.

What has occurred in England and Wales following the Crime and Disorder Act is that practice varies tremendously between different areas. In a very small number of areas, the involvement of victims in restorative justice processes is an important priority, and they are very successful, seeing 70 per cent of victims involved in some form of mediation (Mediation UK 2001). However, these areas are exceptions; most areas involve significantly fewer numbers of victims – around 21 per cent in some way, and just 9 per cent in mediation. The national figure for involving victims is 20 per cent (Dignan 2002). (Several key issues have been identified for this low involvement, which I will come to shortly.) The views of victims who did take part in some form of reparation were that it was a predominantly positive experience. The views of young offenders were that making reparation is positive, and that they clearly accepted that they should be expected to make up for the harm done. Noteworthy is that young offenders felt they had been treated fairly by reparation workers, while they often felt that they had not been by the police and courts (Dignan 2002).

The second piece of legislation is the Youth Justice and Criminal Evidence Act 1999, which went much further than the Crime and Disorder Act, explicitly seeking to introduce a new restorative justice process for some young offenders. From 1 April 2002, all young people who plead guilty at their first appearance in court will either be discharged resulting in the case being dismissed, sentenced to prison if their offending is very serious, or they will receive a Referral Order, which will be the great majority of offenders. Once they have received a Referral Order, they will then have to attend something called a Youth Offender Panel.

The Youth Offender Panel is intended to be a restorative process, similar to a FGC. It will involve the young person and their family, any victims and their supporters, an adviser from the youth offending team, and two members of the local community. These community panel members receive seven days' training. This panel will discuss the offence, and the reasons for the offending. They will agree a contract with the young person, which should include some element of reparation. Depending on the length of the order, which would have been set by the court, the young person will also be required to attend several review panel meetings to look at their progress. If they complete their contract, then their criminal conviction will be considered spent. Unlike the development of FGCs in New Zealand, the majority of young people who attend these panels will be minor offenders. Referral orders have been in operation in 11 of the 154 YOTs in England and Wales for the past 18 months (Newburn *et al.* 2001). They found that 98 per cent of young people agreed contracts at their first panel, with 75 per cent successfully completing their contracts successfully. Less than a quarter (23%) re-offended (Newburn *et al.* 2002). When interviewed, 75 per cent of young offenders and their families expressed that they found the panel useful, and much more memorable and less traumatic than their court appearance (Newburn *et al.* 2002).

Similar to the experience with reparation, the piloting of referral orders has found that very few victims have taken part, approximately 13 per cent among the pilots (Newburn *et al.* 2001). However, the evaluation of the piloting of referral orders found that those that did take part were overwhelmingly positive about their experience. Furthermore, victims who were eligible to take part, but did not, were interviewed. The results from this are illuminating: 50 per cent were never contacted and invited, and 25 per cent were invited but were unable to attend at the time scheduled for the panel. The majority of these indicated that if they had been invited, then they would have attended the panel meeting. Only 25 per cent of victims did not wish to participate (Newburn *et al.* 2001). A number of reasons have been identified for the low involvement of victims in restorative work in England and Wales (Dignan 2002; Holdaway *et al.* 2001; Newburn *et al.* 2001) that relate to difficulties in practice, rather than great reluctance among victims to attend.

Conclusion

This book explores in great detail how restorative practice can be introduced and sustained within educational settings. Almost 30 years of practice experience has shown that restorative justice has much to offer when implemented well, and can be successful in even the most difficult of cases.

Guy Masters
Wandsworth Youth Offending Team

Part I

Introducing the Vision

Anyone working in schools alongside young people today needs vision, commitment and realism. Without vision and commitment it is easy to be worn down by pressures, constant changes and new demands. Without realism it is easy to be set back by the challenges, disappointments and conflicts that are inevitable in the complex whirlwind of the school day. It can feel like a whirlwind when, every day, hundreds and often thousands, of unique individuals struggle to maintain their individuality in a system that, with the best will in the world, cannot accommodate too much individuality!

My vision is to see an ethic of care and an ethic of justice at the heart of the school community. What needs to be in a place for this to happen? By looking at the philosophy, skills and processess summed up in criminal justice circles as 'restorative justice', I consider how this approach could transform the way in which many schools are currently organised. Against a background of the many challenges facing schools today, restorative justice has the potential to make significant contributions in:

- making schools safer, happier places

- reducing exclusion and the need for exclusion

- creating a culture of inclusion and belonging

- raising morale and self-esteem

- raising attendance

- tackling bullying behaviours throughout the school community

- reducing staff turnover and burnout.

There are many community building and community repair initiatives being adopted in schools where people have never heard of the words 'restoratice justice'. Nevertheless, it is within this particular conceptual framework that many apparently disparate initiatives are brought together, perhaps for the first time, as a 'Whole School Approach'.

Chapter 1

Restorative Justice in a School Context

> Restorative Justice is a way to move a child on. For years we've just been containing – putting the lid back on – and eventually that just explodes in your face!
>
> Primary Deputy Head, Banbury

The Introduction gave an overview of restorative justice and the wider context of developments in youth justice. This chapter explains what is new and different about a restorative approach to dealing with challenging behaviour and conflict. It makes the case for focusing on building and repairing relationships rather than on managing and controlling behaviour. Readers are recommended to read this chapter first to gain an overview of the whole concept before considering how to get started in their own school. Later chapters describe restorative skills and how they can be used in a coherent, consistent framework. However, it is important to consider first where you want to end up, whether the vision sketched here is one you share, and in what ways your vision for your own school may be different.

What is restorative justice?

In broad terms restorative justice constitutes an innovative approach to offending and inappropriate behaviour which puts repairing harm done to relationships and people over and above the need for assigning blame and dispensing punishment (Wright 1999). Put even more simply, it is about asking the following questions:

- What happened?
- Who has been affected and how?
- How can we put right the harm?
- What have we all learnt so as to make different choices next time?

The emphasis on 'we' is crucial, because it implies that all those affected by what has happened are also involved in finding the way forward. Contrast this approach with a more traditional one that asks

- What happened?

- Who is to blame?

- What is the appropriate punishment?

and one can begin to see why a restorative approach is, for some people, a completely new way of dealing with a problem.

This approach to justice challenges many notions deeply imbedded in our culture and enacted in many homes, schools and institutions. These notions include the idea that those who do wrong deserve to be punished, that punishment will change behaviour, and that the threat of punishment is required to ensure that potential wrongdoers comply with society's rules.

Howard Zehr, a seminal thinker and writer in this field, once referred to the shift from retributive justice to restorative justice in the arena of criminal justice as a paradigm shift (Zehr 1995). Although he now thinks that they may not be polar opposites, he still recognises that there are significant differences (Zehr 2002). It may be that a similar paradigm shift is needed in a school setting if relationship and behaviour management are to be developed along restorative lines, and more will be said about this in later chapters.

Harm

Thinking about harm can be a useful starting point when considering different ways of dealing with challenging behaviour and conflict (Blood 2000). Most people can relate to being harmed, and to causing harm, at some point in their lives, when harm is defined as 'an adverse effect on another person or people, involving emotional or mental distress and/or physical or material damage'.

If people are asked to consider what they need when they have been harmed the answers tend to be similar:

- someone to listen to my story

- time to calm down

- a chance to ask – Why me? What did I do to deserve that?

- the person concerned to understand and acknowledge the impact their behaviour has had on me

- a sincere, spontaneous apology

- things put right, if possible

- reassurance it won't happen again.

If people are asked what they need when they themselves have caused harm to someone else, whether on purpose or by accident, answers usually include:

- time to think

- someone to listen to my story

- a chance to explain to myself and the other person why I did it

- an opportunity to apologise

- a chance to make amends

- reassurance that the matter is dealt with and I can move on

- hope that there is no resentment left.

More traditional, punitive, approaches to wrongdoing rarely create a situation where the needs expressed above can be met. When a young person behaves in a way that is challenging for a member of staff, for example, there is likely to be harm experienced on both sides unless both people feel heard and understood. There is a possibility that the relationship between the two will be adversely affected, and that will affect the way they work together in the future.

In describing the approach in this way it is clear that restorative justice is driven by a set of values and an ethos that emphasises trust, mutual respect and tolerance. It also acknowledges the importance of human feelings, needs and rights. This value base and ethos needs to underpin behaviour and the various applications of restorative skills. The Restorative Pyramid in Figure 1.1 illustrates this important point.

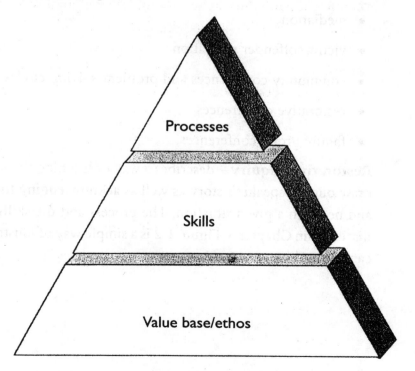

Figure 1.1 The Restorative Pyramid

Restorative processes

The processes and interventions are, in fact, the most public face of restorative justice. They aim to make things as right as possible after some behaviour or event which has adversely affected people. These interventions share certain essential steps. Everyone affected by harmful behaviour, a conflict situation or a problem has the opportunity to talk about what has happened, explain how they have been affected by it, describe how they are currently feeling about the situation and what they want to do to repair the harm caused.

To discuss and explain the processes and the increasingly complex skills they involve I have to adopt a consistent terminology. Some people may prefer other terminology. My position is that it does not matter greatly what we call the processes we are using or in what terms we describe them as long as we hold to the idea that we are exploring and developing a set of generic skills to be applied in different situations, as befits each situation. I have found myself on occasion beginning a process using some of the conventions of restorative conferencing (explained below), and then switching to approaches I recognise from my background in community mediation with a small element of my elementary training in counselling. Flexibility is the key, grounded in an understanding of what we are doing and why we are doing it.

In increasing complexity, because they involve more people, the restorative processes identified and discussed in this book include:

- restorative enquiry
- restorative discussion in challenging situations
- mediation
- victim/offender mediation
- community conferences and problem-solving circles
- restorative conferences
- family group conferences.

Restorative enquiry – describes a way of listening that enables the listener to draw out the speaker's story as well as acknowledging their thoughts, feelings and needs in a given situation. The process and the skills required for this are discussed in Chapter 3. Figure 1.2 is a simple way of illustrating that the process can be used one to one.

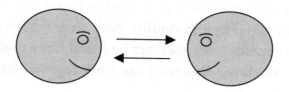

Figure 1.2 Restorative enquiry – a one-to-one process

Restorative discussion in challenging situations – when there might be a power imbalance, such discussion is intended to keep communication flowing so that both sides can express their feelings and needs and achieve mutually acceptable outcomes (Figure 1.3). Power differential, rank or status can be due to any number of factors (including age, position, experience, personality) and can fluctuate during a conversation.

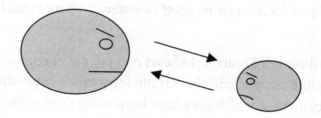

Figure 1.3 Restorative discussion in challenging situations

The term 'restorative discussion' can be a bit of a misnomer since many conversations do not begin because of a harm that needs to be repaired, or because of a relationship that needs to be restored. I like the phrase that Marshall Rosenberg uses – 'nonviolent communication'; it includes any conversation that tries to avoid violence, distress or offence (Rosenberg 1999). I am certainly inspired by his work in this area. However, my sources of inspiration are much wider than his excellent work, and so I am trying to find a way of describing a certain way of relating that keeps channels of communication open, minimises harm where possible and seeks to repair harm if it occurs. An alternative expression could be 'relational discussion' – one that puts the maintenance of the relationship between the two people as a priority. Chapter 4 describes the process and the skills in more detail.

Mediation – a process involving a neutral third party or parties (known as mediators), whose role is to support those in conflict to come to a mutually acceptable resolution, or at least to find a way of moving forward. Figure 1.4 shows two people in conflict, both believing the other IS the problem. Successful outcomes can sometimes be found if the problem is recognised as a shared one, which the disputants can work together on resolving.

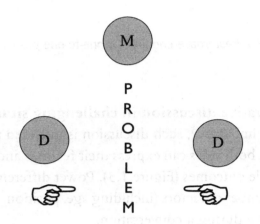

Figure 1.4 A simple model of mediation (M = mediator; D = disputant)

Although Figure 1.4 shows two people in conflict, mediation can be used with more people, and the terminology varies depending on who is talking and the context in which they have been using their skills. This book is going to call the process of addressing conflicts between two people 'mediation' and the process of addressing conflicts between larger groups 'restorative conferences' or 'problem-solving circles', as appropriate. (In Minnesota, where such processes are increasingly used in schools, students and teachers alike simply refer to them all as 'circles'.) Chapter 5 considers mediation in more detail.

Victim/offender mediation – a process significantly different from the previous one in that one person has accepted responsibility, at least to some degree, for the harm caused to the other (see figure 1.5). In criminal cases this person is called the offender. (The words 'victim' and 'offender' are generally inappropriate in a school context and are used here for explanatory purposes only.) A key issue here is to ensure that the process does not re-victimise the victim. Advance preparation, whilst important in any restorative intervention, is vital in such situations so that, as far as possible, there are no surprises in the process. An example of this process in a school might be mediation between someone who has admitted bullying someone else. (Although in my experience the mediators need to be flexible and open to the possibility that the person who has done the bullying might have previously been a victim themselves.) Chapter 5 also reflects on the potential differences between mediation in the event of conflict and victim/offender mediation.

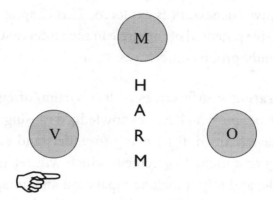

Figure 1.5 Victim/offender mediation – responsibility for harm accepted (M = mediator; V = victim; O = offender)

Community conferences and problem-solving circles – useful when there is a problem to be discussed as a group, a conflict that needs addressing or an event that has caused distress to the whole group (see Figure 1.6). The facilitator has an overall responsibility to ensure the smooth running of the process. However, the group agrees some guidelines at the outset so everyone feels safe and included.

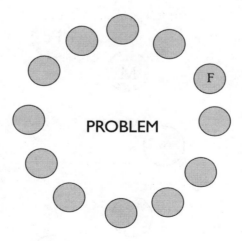

Figure 1.6 A problem-solving circle – discussing a common problem (F = facilitator)

How to prepare for, and use, circles with varying purposes is the focus of Chapters 6 and 7. Chapter 7 considers the circle as a valuable community-building process. It explores how the process itself, as well as the content, can develop people's relational and restorative experience and skills. The process known in the UK as 'circle time' is described and its place in the overall restorative framework is explored. This chapter also looks more closely at the restorative potential of the circle in such interventions as problem-solving circles and family group conferences.

Restorative conferences – like victim/offender mediation, these usually involve people who have acknowledged causing harm in (a) meeting with those they have harmed, (b) seeking to understand each other's perspective and (c) coming to a mutual agreement which will repair the harm caused as much as possible, and might include reparation and an apology.

As explained earlier I use the term 'mediation' to describe the process when it only involves two people and the mediator, and 'conference' to describe a meeting involving more than two people and a mediator. Some schools use the terms 'conference' and 'mini-conference' to distinguish between the two processes. In a conference all sides can bring supporters, who are likely to have been affected and therefore have something to say from a personal perspective. A mini-conference simply involves the two people most directly affected.

Restorative conferences differ from problem-solving circles and family group conferences in that at least one person has acknowledged that they have caused another harm. Chapter 6 discusses the restorative conference and its potential in school in more detail. Figure 1.7 provides an example of a restorative conference.

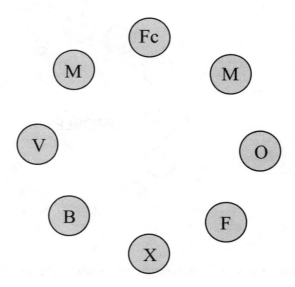

Figure 1.7 One possible make-up of a restorative conference (Fc = facilitator; V = victim; O = offender; M = mother; F = father; B = brother; X = another relevant participant, possibly a member of the school staff)

Family group conferences – useful when a plan is needed to provide support to a young person, or their family in making changes (see Figure 1.8). Family group conferences draw on the strength and resources of a wide extended family network, and are convened in neutral venues by trained, independent co-ordinators. The meeting involves three stages. It starts with professionals sharing information with family members and providing consultancy on options for future help. Then the family members have private time on their own, to discuss and deliberate and come up with a plan for a way forward to help the child's situation. At the end of the meeting key professionals return with the co-ordinator to hear and record the family plan and make arrangements for monitoring and review. This process of family decision making builds responsibility in families, creates a sense of ownership, and motivates those involved to carry out and implement the plans made (Holton 2002). Chapter 6 will make reference to this process.

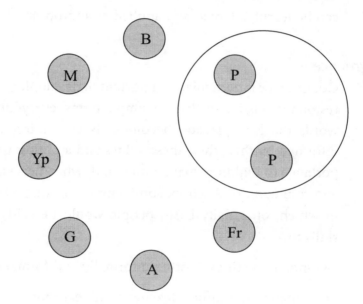

Figure 1.8 A family group conference (B = brother; Yp = young person; G = grandparent; A = aunt; Fr = family friend; P = professional)

Skills and values

The skills required to engage in these processes and interventions include:

- remaining impartial and non-judgemental
- respecting the perspective of all involved
- actively and empathically listening
- developing rapport amongst participants

- empowering participants to come up with solutions rather than suggesting or imposing ideas

- creative questioning

- warmth

- compassion

- patience.

These skills are informed by an intention – namely, to respect the underlying ethos that encompasses the values of respect, openness, empowerment, inclusion, tolerance, integrity and congruence. Every chapter describing a restorative process will give some space to the key skills underpinning that process. It will become clear that, from the everyday casual conversations we have with friends, to the challenging conference aimed at helping a victim and an offender move on from a serious assault, there is a continuum of skills which can be learnt, adapted and applied as appropriate.

Congruence

Congruence is particularly important in developing a whole school approach to restorative justice so that, in simple terms, everyone 'walks the talk'. In other words the key question becomes: 'Is everything we do here at this school informed by this ethos, these values and a philosophy which gives central importance to building, maintaining and, when necessary, repairing relationships and community?' A school community run along restorative lines would be one in which, on a daily basis, people would be using restorative and relational skills to:

- interact with each other informally and formally

- enhance and inform teaching and learning

- have those more challenging conversations

- tackle problems, conflicts and discipline issues (whether these are involving young people or adults)

- structure meetings.

The restorative jigsaw

The underpinning ethos of the approach inspires many different initiatives that seek to involve more of the school community in making decisions about how that community is to run. What makes this book unique is that it considers how all of these initiatives can fit together, like the pieces of a jigsaw, to make a coherent, congruent whole (see figure 1.9). Indeed the central thesis of the book is that it is precisely this whole school approach that is needed if the individual elements are to flourish and achieve their potential. Each one is like the spoke of a wheel, and wheels do not turn smoothly unless each spoke is in place and in good repair.

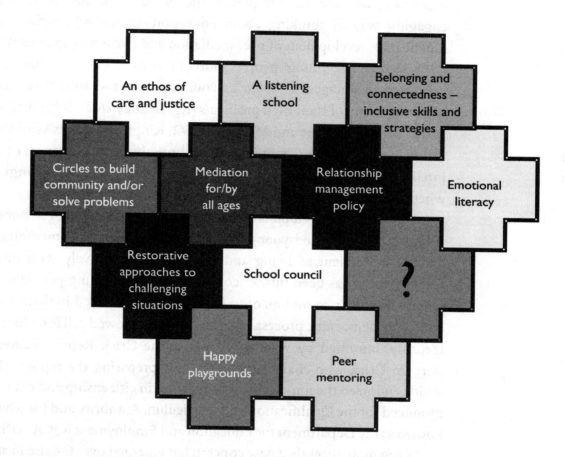

Figure 1.9 Making the pieces fit together – involving the whole school community

I will return to this jigsaw in the final chapter when considering different ways of embarking on a restorative project and the ways in which such projects are evolving currently in the UK.

A brief history

Readers anxious to make a start in exploring the skills and processes that make up restorative justice may want to omit this section. However, others may wish to consider where some of the ideas in this book have come from. What follows is a brief history, from my own perspective as a trainer, consultant, researcher and practitioner in the field of restorative justice in a school setting over the last ten years, and my 12 years as a secondary school teacher before that.

In the late seventies and early eighties many of us talked about 'peace education' and were influenced by the writings of those unhappy with conventional education (e.g. Freire 1982; Holt 1966; Postman and Weingartner 1971;

Reimer 1971). These books were critical of an education system that ignored the rights and needs of individuals and judged people in terms of a limited set of criteria. One risk of such dehumanising was a sense of alienation from what was happening on, and to, our planet; the books advocated a fresh and more engaging way of thinking about education. In the mid-eighties and early nineties the development of peer mediation and circle time gave us the practical tools to involve young people more in their school communities. These processes encouraged us listen to young people and trust their capacity for resolving many of their own problems (e.g. Bentley *et al.* 1998; Bliss, Robinson and Maires 1995; Fine and Macbeth 1992; Kingston Friends Workshop Group 1996; Mosley 1993). The mid-nineties brought us an awareness of emotional intelligence and of the importance of being in touch with our feelings and needs when resolving conflicts (Goleman 1996; Rosenberg 1999).

Many of the developments mentioned above grew out of a concern for developing well-rounded young people with self-esteem, communication skills and a commitment to living and working co-operatively with others. More recently there has been further concern to develop young people's social conscience and their commitment to being actively involved in their communities and in the democratic process. This has led to a renewed call for education in citizenship, informed by what is known as the Crick Report, named after Sir Bernard Crick who chaired the committee preparing the report. This report, which endorsed the importance of education in citizenship and democracy, was produced for the Qualification and Curriculum Authority and for what was then known as the Department for Education and Employment (QCA/DfEE 1998).

Even more recently a new concern has emerged over the rise in street crime and over increasingly challenging behaviour from young people both inside and outside school. Police officers are being assigned to work regularly in some schools to support teachers working in challenging situations. A very recent development is the publication of a set of protocols for developing safer schools, produced by a partnership involving the Department for Education and Employment, the Home Office, the Youth Justice Board, the Association of Chief Education Officers (ACEO) and the Association of Chief Police Officers (ACPO). This initiative is called the Safer Schools Partnership (SSP) project. Both the Crick Report and the Safer Schools Partnership draft guidance emphasise the need for greater involvement on the part of young people in the organisation of their school community and the need for conflict management and relational skills to help them to do this. The Crick Report endorses mediation, conflict management and circle time (all of which will be considered in more depth in later chapters). The Safer Schools guidance advocates developing more restorative practices in schools. This mainstream endorsement of ideas that in the seventies were slightly marginal, and possibly even somewhat 'alternative', highlights the point that restorative justice, as a philosophy, a set of skills and a toolbox of applications, is 'an idea whose time has come', as Keith Bradley from the Home Office phrased it in the autumn of 2001.

Summary

In setting the scene for the whole book, Chapter 1 briefly described the definition of restorative justice to be used. It outlined the restorative processes and skills that are going to be described, and briefly touched on what a whole school restorative approach might look like. It set this approach in the context of other educational developments in the field of relationships and behaviour management over the past 20 years or so. This was not an exhaustive treatment of this issue, nor did it consider the development in approaches to behaviour management in schools over the past few hundred years. That would be a fascinating study in itself and may well parallel approaches to developments in the criminal justice system and, in particular, attitudes to punishment. One of the contributions restorative justice can make in a school is to raise the awareness of the wider community about alternative approaches to punishment, and perhaps create a less vengeful and retributive society.

There are many different ways of introducing restorative justice into a school. Different schools have different needs, and change can happen for different reasons. It is a central thesis of this book that the essential seeds of restorative philosophy and approach are contained in each aspect of the restorative jigsaw and that, wherever and however one starts, the seeds of change will be planted and will, with support and commitment, grow into other areas of the school.

Chapter 2

Bringing People on Board and Establishing the Vision

Running an Introductory Workshop

> A key ingredient to school success is the extent to which the values of school life are shared among all the members of the community. Life outside may be very different, but in school there is a code of conduct and of behaviour which all try to sustain in their dealings with each other and the outside world. (Brighouse and Woods 2000, p.55)

Before embarking on a project that will involve everyone in a school community, it is advisable to consult with as many people as possible in that community. This is congruent with the restorative principle of inclusion and of involving those affected by an issue to have a say in finding a way forward. This chapter describes several ways in which one can engage people in the project at the outset. It is a practical chapter with advice on how to run an introductory workshop. It is also theoretical, in that it explains the key values underpinning a restorative project and the way in which these relate to the values held already by members of a school community.

Change changes people

It might be tempting to wish for a magic wand, a quick fix that would change all the individuals in an organisation overnight, so that one morning the ethos, the commitment, the systems, the skills and the time for restorative interventions would all miraculously be in place. But in fact this would be to miss the point. The journey to change is what changes people! Transforming a school, or indeed any organisation, to a place where restorative justice informs the way people interact daily with each other needs to be done restoratively. Everyone who will be affected by the changes needs to be involved and feel that their views are being respected and taken into consideration.

Restorative values

The value base of a restorative approach draws inspiration from many sources but includes the following elements:

- mutual respect and appreciation

- a belief in people's ability to resolve their own problems given time, support and a chance to tell their story

- acceptance of diversity

- an inclusive approach to problem-solving, so that the feelings, needs and views of everyone in a given community are taken into account

- congruence between beliefs and actions – 'walking the talk'.

Using restorative interventions to repair harm in a school community that does not embrace restorative values will have a limited effect on those involved. The interventions may even be counterproductive if those involved in such an intervention are treated in one way by the restorative practitioners and in a different way by others in the community. The progress made can be nullified by conflicting messages and thoughtless remarks. The preparation, the restorative process itself and the subsequent ongoing support of those involved need to be done in a restorative way if there is to be lasting benefit. Members of the school community have an important role to play in this process, as will be explored more fully. Furthermore, a school community run along restorative lines may need fewer restorative interventions to repair harm.

The purpose of the introductory workshop is to provide some information and, much more importantly, to create a bridge between what people in a school community are doing at present and what they would like to be doing in the future. Establishing common ground and aligning a restorative project with people's current values and beliefs sets the scene for a shared journey to a shared goal.

Finding common ground in the circle: The introductory workshop

It is recommended that most of the issues discussed below be explored by participants sitting in an open circle. Circles are at the heart of restorative processes, since there is an opportunity for everyone to feel involved, as equals, and have an equal opportunity to speak if certain conventions are followed. If the numbers are too large for one circle then it is often possible to organise smaller circles round the room. In this case clear instructions would need to be given so that each circle can run itself in a way that is inclusive, safe and respectful.

The use of circles in staff, team and class meetings is explored in more detail in Chapter 7. The process is a key one for developing skills and creating a supportive environment, and as such it is useful to give people an experience of its usefulness right from the very beginning.

Certain circle conventions can be suggested so that what might be a first experience of this way of working is a positive one. It cannot be emphasised strongly enough that restorative practice is as much about HOW one does something as WHAT one does. Process and content are inextricably linked. As a minimum set of guidelines I suggest:

- Each circle has a facilitator whose role is to ensure that the circle runs smoothly and that the guidelines are respected.

- Everyone has the opportunity to contibute, in turn, round the circle.

- Everyone waits their turn to speak and does not cut in whilst someone else is speaking or before their turn.

- Everyone has the right to keep silent and 'pass'.

The following sequence of questions gives people a chance to share their values, sometimes for the first time as a group, and relate them to restorative practice. The order in which they appear here is usually the order in which I would introduce them in an introductory workshop with a school. Most of the questions can be explored with people of any age, although the language may need to be changed for younger people.

Introductions

Before embarking on the questions I would ensure that people know each other by inviting introductions round the circle or circles. It is sometimes appropriate to ask what questions people have come with and what they hope to get out of the session. These can be written on a flipchart and referred back to at the end of the session.

A very short introduction about restorative justice, including the Restorative Pyramid model (Figure 1.1 in Chapter 1), helps to set the scene for exploring what is at the base of the pyramid – the ethos and value base. This is the focus of what is to follow.

Establishing an effective working environment

The members of a school community have strong ideas about what they need from each other to work at their best, and whether or not they are getting these needs met. The question

What do you need from others to work at your best?

can be an important starting point at the outset of any restorative project.

Answers from adults, initially elicited from people talking in pairs, and then by inviting contributions from each pair round the circle, include:

- someone to listen to me

- the sharing of ideas and resources

- an acceptance that it is OK to make mistakes

- encouragement

- praise and thanks for a job well done

- constructive feedback

- enough time and information to do a job properly

- practical and emotional support when I need it

- a sense of humour

- being included and made to feel I belong.

In my experience the answers from young people are similar. The findings can be written up on a flipchart, board or screen for everyone to see.

The ensuing discussion can be interesting because the questions are framed in such a way that it emphasises 'needs' and 'others'. This question implies that if people do not get what they need, they are not working at their best. Furthermore it implies a personal responsibility to support each other.

A useful second step is to invite everyone present to take ownership of a smaller, essential, list by choosing the three most important things they need 'without which they would not be able to function effectively'. Brightly coloured sticky dots can be distributed amongst the group, or coloured felt tips, and everyone can be invited to 'make their mark'. Dots or ticks cluster round certain key words, and, in essence, this highlights what the group needs and values in their relationships with each other.

In my experience, and I have done this activity hundreds of times, with disparate groups around the country, what most people need, and therefore value, is:

- co-operation through emotional and practical support

- mutual respect and trust

- a willingness to listen to one another

- a culture of encouragement

- feeling as if they belong to the team/group/class.

Practical steps to meeting people's needs

It is one thing to identify the value base and needs of a group and another to ensure that the needs expressed are met. In simple terms, it can sometimes boil down to whether, as individuals, the members of a group are providing these things for each other, or have opportunities to do so.

An exploration of what this can mean in practice can be teased out by inviting people each to take the various elements of the essential list and complete a sentence about them in turn round the circle. This circle-time activity, called 'sentence completion' (Bliss *et al.* 1995), can be used to address serious topics with a relatively light touch. If time is short this extension of the activity could be left until another occasion.

I prefer to do one example, if I possibly can, since it does demonstrate the power of the process and gets people thinking. A good one for an introductory workshop is:

I don't feel respected when...

This 'go round' has elicited responses such as:

- a colleague/teacher shouts at me in front of other students

- my authority is undermined by a senior colleague

- my opinion is not asked for

- my opinion is ignored when given

- someone does not look at me when I am speaking

- my effort is never acknowledged.

The depth of feeling when this issue is explored can be surprising. It is also important to give people an opportunity to describe when they do feel respected. Adults and children alike need to know what to do, as well as what not to do.

I do feel respected when...

can elicit such responses as:

- people ask for my opinion and value it

- people greet me by my name

- someone says they will do something for me, and they keep their word

- my questions are valued and answered where possible

- I am kept informed about things I need to know to do my job.

This sharing of experiences and needs promotes discussion about very practical measures that can be taken, either as individuals or as a group.

The point about this exploration is that people tend to have similar needs and share similar values about how a group functions at its best. Restorative practice grows out of these essentially human values. This is an important point to establish at the outset. The reason restorative practices make sense to people is that they allow us to interact in the way we want to, and need to, as human beings.

Rule making and rule breaking

Exploring what the people in a community need from each other creates a template for a set of accepted guidelines for behaviour. These are not rules imposed from the top, but guidelines developed democratically across the community. Looking more closely at the needs expressed, it would appear that, in order to work at our best, we need to feel safe, happy, valued and included. These needs contribute not just to our ability to work but to our general well-being. If we do not get our needs met our well-being is at stake. Using restorative terminology, we may well be on the receiving end of harmful behaviour. The onus is on every member of the community to be mindful of the guidelines, to take responsibility to adhere to them, and to acknowledge that failure to adhere to them may necessitate a restorative process to repair the harm done and to make amends. How a school community makes its rules, to whom these rules apply and how rule breaking is addressed are key issues in developing a whole school restorative approach.

What are we here for?

Just as every member of a school community has strong ideas about their own personal needs they usually have views on the school's purpose. Many teachers come into the teaching profession with high ideals and expectations. Over the years conflicting pressures can erode the idealism and teacher burnout is a very real issue. Similarly, many young people look forward to starting school and yet over the years become disillusioned and often disaffected. What on earth is going wrong? Reconnecting with the vision can be energising and also instructive.

One question that can engage the adults in a school community is:

What do you want young people to leave this school with in terms of skills, values and attitudes?

Answers from around the country tend to be similar and include:

- a belief in self
- a sense of responsibility to self and others
- emotional literacy

- self-awareness
- ability to get on with others
- curiosity
- openness to others' ideas
- a sense of humour
- resilience
- a positive outlook on life
- tolerance of differences
- knowing how to learn
- realistic expectations of self and others.

Frustration can set in when teachers see a disparity between what they think education is about and what they are expected to do on a day-to-day basis. Whilst acknowledging the importance of academic achievement and basic key skills, many teachers believe that the emphasis on national targets and league tables has created a situation where the real purpose of education has got lost. I have heard much frustration expressed at the lack of time for developing the skills and attitudes listed above, important though teachers believe them to be. Training in restorative and relational skills and participating in restorative processes can help develop these skills and attitudes.

I might not ask exactly the same question to young people – it is quite a sophisticated one. However, young people are often clear about what they want from their school experience. This in itself suggests their wider agenda of what they wish to get out of it, not in academic terms but in terms of their own personal growth and development.

A presentation by young people in 2002 to the All Party Parliamentary Group for Children (APPGC 2002) conveyed the message:

- we want to learn
- we want a curriculum that is more flexible
- we want more choice in the things we study
- we want to be treated with respect
- we want to be treated as individuals
- we want to be involved in decisions that affect us
- we want more say in how our schools are run
- we need schools to be safe places

- we need teachers to do more than just teach; we want them to understand young people, to care what happens to us

- we need support when we have difficulties, not punishment

- we need help to stay in school

- we need you to do something about it.

It would appear that there is a lot of common ground between teachers and young people about what is important about the school experience. The challenge is to incorporate the values, skills and opportunities into the equally important task of delivering an academic curriculum that equips young people for the future and provides them with the qualifications they need.

In fact the National Curriculum guidelines and the Key Stage descriptors do provide opportunities for developing many of the things mentioned above. One of the problems is the increasingly narrow focus on exams and tests. There does seem to be a mismatch between the Standards Agenda on the one hand and the Inclusion Agenda on the other. The Standards Agenda is putting pressure on schools to achieve academic targets or else sink down the national league tables. Any young person who is not part of the academic success solution because of their behaviour is often labelled as part of the problem, and one strategy is to exclude them, or refuse them entry into the school in the first place.

The Inclusion Agenda is encouraging schools to address the needs of all young people, providing not only a relevant academic education for everyone, regardless of background or ability, but also developing their emotional, moral, social and spiritual welfare. The importance of educating the whole child is recognised within the Inclusion Agenda, and yet apparently is not a high priority on the Standards Agenda. Ironically, the pressure to comply with the Standards Agenda is creating more unrest and more behaviour problems in school,s making it harder for schools to comply with the Inclusion Agenda. If neither teachers nor students feel they are getting their needs met, or that their vision of what school is really for is being realised, then dissatisfaction, disaffection and demoralisation can set in. (Cremin 2002c)

A whole school restorative approach can provide opportunities for teachers to develop in themselves, and in young people, the skills that they value as central to lifelong learning. Young people, for their part, can see the point of learning such skills, and relish the chance to be more involved. The approach has the potential to meet all the needs expressed by those young people who addressed the All Party Parliamentary Group for Children.

Many teachers have been struck by the strategies and experiential techniques used in restorative skills training courses and used them to transform their teaching style as well as the way they address behavioural issues.

Creating a template for change

What follows is an energising activity designed to highlight key elements that might be missing in a community in crisis, and what needs to be in place to turn things around (adapted with permission from the Kingston Friends Workshop Group (1996)). Once again it is based on what people have experienced and what they dream of. It provides a template for the future development of the project and provides a rationale for the training style and content. The following question is asked, and written where everyone can see it:

What happens in the classroom or the staff room on a really bad day?

It is useful to elicit suggestions from people working first in pairs, one concentrating on the staff room (if the group includes people who use the staff room) and one on the classroom. First, people are invited to draw a simple iceberg shape on a plain piece of paper. Next they are invited to consider either a staff room they have known or a classroom they have known and, using neutral description only, write what they might see or hear in that room on a very bad day, ABOVE the water line (see Figure 2.1). In other words, the focus is the 'staff room or classroom from hell' scenario.

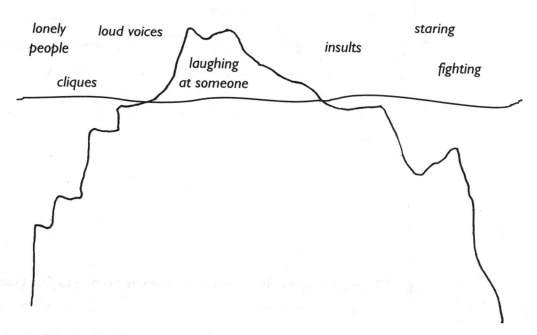

Figure 2.1 Iceberg diagram for a negative school environment – surface traits

Once both people in the pair have had a chance to consider their particular environment they are invited to share their drawings. A brief discussion can then be held with the group as to whether or not there are similarities between the two drawings. A frequently made observation is that in a classroom young people are often more overt in their negative behaviour and adults in a staff room are more covert, but that similar needs and feelings are being expressed in different ways.

The pictures are usually essentially similar and ideas can be sought around the group for writing on the flipchart drawing. People tend to agree that the description is one of an extremely uncomfortable and unsafe space.

The activity is then repeated, on a fresh diagram, with the two people swapping focus, so that the person who was considering a staff room thinks of a classroom of their acquaintance and vice versa. The question this time is:

What happens, or what would you like to happen, in the classroom or the staff room on a really good day?

Once again, when both partners have had time for individual reflection and writing, the drawings are compared and discussed. There is usually enough similarity for a shared picture to be created on a flipchart sheet with contributions from around the room.

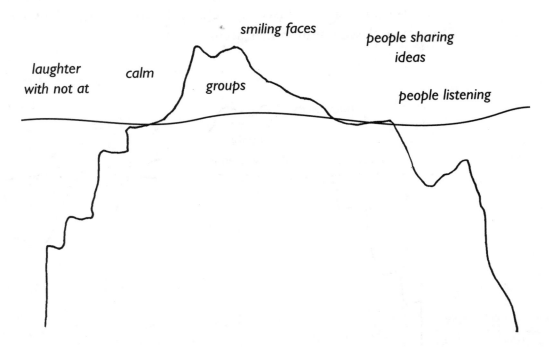

Figure 2.2 Iceberg diagram for a positive school environment – surface traits

This time there is general agreement that this environment feels much safer and it is often possible to link the picture back to the guidelines about what people need to work at their best. The second picture epitomises this ideal working environment.

At this stage it is useful to return to the first drawing and reveal that the drawing is that of an iceberg, with its associations of cold and uninviting environment. It is also worth making the point that what one sees is just the tip of the iceberg and that underneath the surface there is much more going on. By pointing out the negative aspects of the picture it is possible to suggest that in such an environment people are unlikely to be working well together. This might be through a lack of willingness, a lack of skill or simply because sharing ideas is risky or not encouraged. Instead people either do not feel that their ideas are valuable or else want to keep them to themselves in an attempt to get one over on their mates. The phrase 'lack of co-operation' can be written just beneath the surface of the water.

Does such an environment make it difficult for people to express themselves and listen properly to others? Or is it in fact the case that people lack the skills and the opportunities to communicate properly and this leads to the lack of safety and trust? Daniel Goleman (1996) would argue that we all need certain emotional competencies to be emotionally literate:

- knowing one's emotions

- managing one's emotions

- motivating oneself

- recognising emotions in others

- handling emotions.

I would add that the ability to express these emotions, to hear them expressed by others and to respond with empathy are also important skills for the emotionally literate person. The absence of such skills would certainly not help create a safe environment. These skills are considered in more detail in Chapters 3 and 4.

With agreement from the group I would write the phrase 'lack of communication' below 'lack of co-operation', whilst making the point that time and space to use the skills are as important as the skills themselves. People often complain that communication is bad in an organisation because no time is made for it.

In an environment where there is little team spirit, little co-operation and limited communication at any level, the chances are that morale is low and so is the self-esteem of many of the people in the group in question. Furthermore, there is little sense of community or belonging. Once again one can wonder whether low self-esteem is contributing to the problem or a consequence of it. I find general agreement that young people with low self-esteem lack appropriate social skills and therefore often try to make friends or get attention in inappropriate ways. Many people engaging in bullying behaviour, young and old, are suffering from low self-esteem.

As for factors impacting on low self-esteem, my own experience in working in schools preparing for, or recovering from, OFSTED inspections is that these events can seriously affect morale and self-esteem. Tension, stress, worry and self-doubt can easily spread from adults to young people and lead to conflict and disruption. People can feel isolated in these negative emotions, unable to admit what they are feeling for fear of being labelled as inadequate.

In other words, low self-esteem can cause disharmony, disruption and isolation, whilst external disruption of one sort or another can lower self-esteem, increase the sense of isolation and lead to disharmony. In this environment it is rare for people to express appreciation of others openly, and people do not feel valued. Again with permission from the group I would write the phrase 'lack of self-esteem' at the base of the iceberg and also the word 'disconnectedness'. A sense of isolation and unbelonging, of being disconnected from other people, goes hand in hand with low self-esteem, as key factors behind everything else already identified in the iceberg. (The importance of belonging is a central theme through the book, and recent research on school connectedness is discussed in more detail in Chapter 8.) I might also add 'lack of appreciation of others' since those with low self-esteem are often unable to give others positive feedback. (See Figure 2.3.)

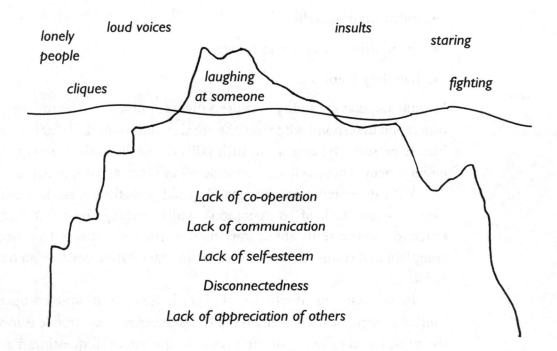

Figure 2.3 Iceberg diagram for a negative school environment – surface traits and their underlying causes

After some discussion it is useful to hypothesise that a more positive environment can be created by focusing on what is beneath the surface of the water and developing co-operation skills and opportunities to use them, communication skills and the time and space to use them, and committing the school to a policy of building and maintaining the self-esteem of adults and students alike (see Figure 2.4). In writing the positive elements beneath the water it can be useful to reflect that the iceberg will now feel warmer, and has perhaps turned into a solid mountain with firm foundations. (The metaphor is a little contrived, since a real iceberg would melt as it warms up, but the iceberg and the mountain are both images people can relate to in their own right so I find people are willing to suspend disbelief.)

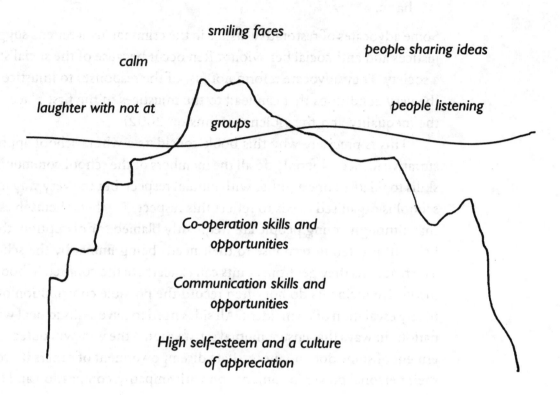

smiling faces

people sharing ideas

calm

laughter with not at

groups

people listening

Co-operation skills and opportunities

Communication skills and opportunities

High self-esteem and a culture of appreciation

Figure 2.4 Iceberg diagram for a positive school environment – surface traits and their underlying causes

Perhaps the iceberg/mountain model helps to explain why creating a climate of mutual respect, though almost universally identified as a need, is nevertheless a challenge in many schools. Adults need to feel respected and valued and to have high self-esteem to be able to respect, value and affirm their students effectively. Creating opportunities for everyone to feel heard, included and acknowledged can help develop a sense of belonging and boost self-esteem. Chapter 7 looks at ways of doing this across the school community starting with 'circles'. As will become clear, addressing conflicts, problems and anti-social behaviour in a restorative way is another way to ensure that everyone feels valued. The chapters on restorative skills and processes explore how to do this.

Power, empowerment and disempowerment

A final word needs to be said about the potential of a restorative approach to empower people in the school community to:

- take more responsibility for their actions

- share the responsibility for deciding how to resolve problems and repair harm.

Some advocates of restorative justice in the criminal justice arena suggest that injustices and anti-social behaviour often occur because of the social structures of a society. They advocate reform not just of the responses to injustice but also of the very conditions that can lead to the injustices in the first place – the harm, the inequality and the violence (Johnston 2002).

This is precisely why this book considers a whole school approach to restorative justice. Not only do all the members of the school community need the skills to relate to one another with mutual respect, but the very way in which the school is organised needs to reflect this respect. Teachers themselves will admit that although young people are frequently blamed for disruption, their 'misbehaviour' is often in response to their needs being unmet by the school system. The reactions they get from adults can exacerbate the conflict. School records of disruptive incidents do not often record the possible contribution of the adults to any escalation of an incident. All sides need to have skills to deal with such situations in ways that ensure mutual satisfaction – the win-win outcome. Empowerment of some does not necessitate disempowerment of others if everyone uses their personal power in conjunction with empathy, compassion and responsibility.

Voicing concerns

At the beginning of the chapter it was stressed how important it is to consult with as many people as possible, to explain the relevance of restorative approaches to their current situation, and to allow for questions and concerns. The last part of an introductory workshop must create opportunities for the expression of doubts, fears and reservations. If these are ignored the project will not be truly restorative and indeed could create conflicts instead.

This is a delicate situation because it is also unwise to end a presentation on a negative note. The following activity, developed after working with Jerry Tyrrell in Northern Ireland (Tyrrell 2002), allows for both the 'No' and the 'Yes' voices to be heard.

YES BUT/NO BUT

What follows would come at the end of an introductory workshop such as the one described in this chapter, a workshop supplemented perhaps by some live demonstrations or video clips of various restorative interventions.

I would invite everyone to identify with a member of the school community: to put on this person's hat and see the world through their eyes for a minute. The first stage is to identify the different constituents of the community:

- senior management

- classroom teachers

- classroom assistants

- students

- parents

- governors

- lunchtime controllers

- office staff

- caretakers

- cleaning staff

- canteen staff

- behavioural support staff.

Those present may suggest other categories. (It is possible that all of these constituencies are in fact represented in the audience. Even so, an invitation to look through another set of eyes might be instructive and fun.)

The second stage is to invite people to reconsider the various processes and applications of restorative skills they have seen. It can be helpful to have these displayed in picture form for all to see (Figures 1.2–1.8 in Chapter 1). Ideally there will be enough people in the group to team up and flesh out their characters a little. The group of students can be of different ages, stages and personalities for example, so different perspectives can be heard.

In their groups people are invited to be as negative as possible about the various processes and come up with every reason they can think of why these, and indeed the whole project, would not work in their school. These answers are then collected round the circle and written on a flipchart. The activity gives permission for all the doubts and fears to be expressed – and they will be recorded and considered in due course. Issues raised include:

- Lack of resources – e.g. money for training and staff cover.

- Lack of time to deal with problems restoratively.

- All very well – but my staff/parents need to feel supported and to know that something is being done. I need to be seen to be tough. (headteacher)

- Won't work – no one ever listens to us. (student)

- What if people refuse to co-operate? (teacher/lunchtime supervisor)

- I don't have any problems – my students know who is boss. (teacher)

- In my day there were not problems like this – we need more discipline, not less. (parent/governor)

Although the feedback can be disheartening it is imperative that the facilitator does not try to address the problems at this stage. Providing there is a mandate to continue then many of the problems will get addressed and resolved by the school itself along the way.

The atmosphere in the workshop at this stage feels a bit scary:

- Change is scary.

- Changing one's behaviour is scary.

- Being asked to give up tried and tested strategies, even if they have not been very successful, is scary.

- Being asked to give up strategies you believe to have been successful, and hear someone else imply that they have not been successful in the long term because the problems surface elsewhere, is not only scary, it is insulting.

- Being asked to consider keeping in school the challenging, disruptive students you want to see the back of, by trying something you as yet feel sceptical about, is scary.

- Refraining from persuasion at this point as a facilitator is scary…!

However, a key restorative principle is that it is the people with the problems who are best placed to resolve them and come up with solutions. What happens next is a practical demonstration of a problem-solving circle.

A metaphorical magic wand is waved and people are invited to imagine they have had a miraculous change of heart. They are asked to consider how their characters could benefit from such an initiative. A new list is created and, by referring to the various restorative processes, each group is invited to think positively. What happens is that often the very problems identified in the first round are addressed and suggestions are given to resolve them. Students feel hopeful that maybe at last teachers will see things from their point of view as well. Teachers look forward to learning more effective strategies for dealing with challenging situations. Headteachers see possibilities for a more harmonious community and for reducing exclusion. Parents wonder if they can have training in dealing with conflicts at home with their children. The mood changes and there is usually an air of excitement and anticipation. There is a mandate to move on to the next stage – training key individuals in the skills so that these can be shared across the school community. This initial cohort of trainees may become part of a school steering group; this is discussed in greater detail in Chapter 9.

The workshop can end with a final go-round in each circle, everyone completing a sentence such as:

One thought/new idea I am going to take away with me today is...

Summary

This chapter has described some practical ways in which to begin exploring key restorative values with members of a school community. It has described how to run certain activities – the process – as well as what could be included – the content – on the grounds that congruence of process and content are fundamental restorative values.

By asking the following questions

- What do you need from others to work at your best?

- What do you want young people to leave this school with in terms of skills, values and attitudes?

- What happens in the classroom or the staff room on a really bad day?

- What happens, or what would you like to happen, in the classroom or the staff room on a really good day?

the chapter explains how one can elicit a vision of the baseline for any restorative organisation.

The baseline identified by the four questions is what would need to be restored in the event of disharmony, conflict or disruption. Restorative justice is predicated on the notion of repairing the harm caused to relationship and community by conflict and anti-social behaviour. The assumption is that there needs to be something to repair. People need to care about each other to want to repair harm. Restorative justice, as explained in the first chapter, is about establishing that ethos of care as well as an ethos of justice into a school.

By giving space for doubts and concerns the message is conveyed that there are different views and perspectives that need to be taken into consideration. This is a key restorative problem-solving principle. The problems raised will not be brushed under the carpet. They will be recorded and addressed as the project develops.

The following chapters will move on to develop the skills needed to build and repair relationships, suggest their applications in the school setting and provide the building blocks for the whole school restorative approach.

Part II

Restorative Skills and Processes

A restorative process enables people in conflict, or between whom there is a rift because of harm done by either side, to sit down together, to listen to each other's perspective on what happened, to hear how everyone is feeling, to hear how everyone has been affected by the situation, to hear what everyone would like to see happen to put the matter right as far as possible and to agree to a plan of action, which might begin by remorse and apology being expressed where appropriate.

Restorative processes can require one or two facilitators, or they can be managaed by the people involved. They work best if the people present are there of their own free will. Although the agreements are not legally binding they are the stronger for being agreed by everyone present, rather then being imposed.

The keys to a successful restorative process are preparation, planning, patience and ongoing support and commitment to the agreement after the process.

The following chapters focus on restorative processes of increasing complexity, beginning with the simplest, and perhaps the most challenging - the day-to-day interactions we have, as individuals, with each other. I call these restorative discussions and conversations, not necessarily because when they begin they are restoring something that has been lost, but because they are intentionally maintianing relationships and connections and therefore draw on the skills I am choosing to call 'restorative'.

Chapter 3

Becoming a Listening School

Restorative approaches in school means everyone has a chance to be heard and they provide opportunities for healing.

Administrative Assistant in a secondary school

This chapter focuses on the basic building block of all restorative processes – the art of active, empathic listening. It considers what this means in practice, how the skills can be developed and why becoming a listening school is a vital first step on the path to a whole school restorative approach. It also describes the process of restorative enquiry, a vital part of all restorative interventions, which has many applications in a school context.

Fortunately for the reader who has yet to get the support of the wider community of their school, empathic listening and restorative enquiry can be used by any individual wanting to make a difference in their classroom with their students, with their classmates or in their team. Even individuals acting differently can begin to make a difference, and although it can feel like an uphill struggle at times, people do notice and can begin to change as well.

Active, empathic listening

Listening with empathy and without overt judgement is the key to connection with another person and is one of the hardest things to do, especially when the other person may well not be giving you this quality listening. It sometimes feels as if active listeners have to do the job of two people. On the one hand they are refraining, in the first instance, from putting across their own point of view and their own feelings and thoughts on the matter being discussed. On the other hand they are acknowledging and perhaps articulating the thoughts and feelings of the other person, which may be coming across in a garbled and accusatory fashion. This takes a great deal of restraint and skill.

There are several key restorative beliefs underpinning active listening and these guide what I would call the intention of the restorative practitioner:

1. Valuing the speaker.

2. Curiosity.

3. Feelings matter.

4. Self-awareness.

5. Win-win.

1. Valuing the speaker. The first and most important belief is that the speaker is a worthwhile person, and has the right to be listened to and taken seriously. If people do not feel heard they will carry on repeating themselves in different ways until they do feel heard (Stone, Patton and Heen 1999). Furthermore, if people do not feel heard they will probably not be in a position to hear others. From a pragmatic point of view, one is more likely to get an opportunity to express one's own story if this has happened, and to have the story heard and appreciated.

2. Curiosity. There is no one 'Truth' about a given situation; there are only 'Truths' (Stone *et al.* 1999). In other words, everyone has their own experience of a situation, just like in 'The Six Blind Men and the Elephant', and this is their truth.

The Six Blind Men and the Elephant

It was six men of Indostan
    To learning much inclined
Who went to see the Elephant
    (Though all of them were blind),
That each by observation
    Might satisfy his mind

The First approached the Elephant,
    And happening to fall
Against his broad and sturdy side,
    At once began to bawl:
'God bless me! but the Elephant
    Is very like a wall!'

The Second, feeling of the tusk,
    Cried 'Ho! what have we here
So very round and smooth and sharp?
    To me 'tis mighty clear
This wonder of an Elephant
    Is very like a spear!'

The Third approached the animal,
    And happening to take
The squirming trunk within his hands,
    Thus boldly up and spake:
'I see,' quoth he, 'the Elephant
    Is very like a snake!'

The Fourth reached out an eager hand,
    And felt about the knee
'What most his wondrous beast is like
    Is mighty plain,' quoth he;
''Tis clear enough the Elephant
    Is very like a tree!'

The Fifth, who chanced to touch the ear,
    Said 'E'en the blindest man
Can tell what this resembles most;
    Deny the fact who can
This marvel of an Elephant
    Is very like a fan!'

The Sixth no sooner had begun
    About the beast to grope
Than, seizing on the swinging tail
    That fell within his scope,
'I see,' quoth he, 'the Elephant
    Is very like a rope!'

And so these men of Indostan
    Disputed loud and long,
Each in his own opinion
    Exceeding still and strong,
Though each was partly in the right,
    And all were in the wrong!

Moral:

So oft in theologic wars;
    The disputants, I ween,
Rail on in utter ignorance
    Of what each other mean,
And prate about an Elephant
    Not one of them has seen!

John Godfrey Saxe (1816–1887)

The key is for the listener to be curious about how others see the same situation, invite them to tell their story and acknowledge their right to a different point of view.

3. Feelings matter. A feeling is a feeling, and although feelings can change, there is no intrinsically 'right' or 'wrong' way to feel about something. Acknowledging the way someone else is feeling, or at least expressing interest in how they might be feeling, can be very important in making a connection.

4. Self-awareness. Our thoughts, feelings, needs and behaviour are inextricably linked, and at any given time these will be influencing each other (see Figure 3.1). What we believe and think about a given situation will affect how we are feeling. How we are feeling will impact on what we do next, and this is likely to be driven by what we need at that point. How we interpret another's reaction to what we do will trigger other feelings and other needs – and so on (Margetts 2002; Rosenberg 1999). The key to a creative and positive outcome in a discussion is to remain in touch with the stories we are telling, with our feelings and our needs, and to be able to express these to ourselves in the first instance, and then to those with whom we are talking. In essence this is giving ourselves first the empathy we need to give to others.

'The Six Blind Men and the Elephant' sums up this notion of interdependent aspects of our experience and relates also to the importance of valuing each other, being curious and respecting feeling. By acknowledging that inside everyone these interdependent aspects are at work we are able to understand, respect and value each other as thinking, feeling human beings with needs. This is a key idea, and will be referred to frequently in elaborating restorative skills and processes in ensuing chapters.

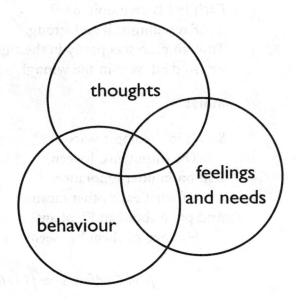

Figure 3.1 The interrelationship between thoughts, feelings, needs and behaviour

5. Win-win. The most desirable outcomes of a difficult conversation are those in which all sides can find a mutually acceptable outcome or at least find a way to cope with the situation as it is. Sometimes solutions are not available and some things cannot be changed, but the ability to cope and to hope can be positive outcomes in themselves.

However skilled one is as a listener, and whatever skills one uses, the starting point needs to be one of intention. To listen in a way that either builds, maintains or repairs a relationship between two or more people requires a sense of curiosity and open-mindedness, respect for different points of view and a commitment to keeping the conversation flowing. Marshall Rosenberg has a wonderful expression – 'Words can be windows or walls' (Rosenberg 1999).

The intention behind a restorative conversation is to ensure that one's words are windows and not walls.

Developing essential skills

What follows is a reflection on some of the essential skills of active listening. The intention is to stimulate thought and self-appraisal on the part of you, the reader, and to encourage review of the current status of listening within a school. Readers are encouraged to supplement their own development by dipping into the references list at the end of the book; many of these titles have been sources of inspiration in the approach described here.

Body language

It is often said that body language speaks louder than words, and whilst words can be windows or walls so body language too can send powerful messages. In counselling training the expression 'open body language' is used to describe a particular set of behaviours that conveys to a speaker that the listener is really listening. In a training situation the invitation to sit as though you were really interested in what the trainer is saying can be responded to by participants of all ages, from the very young to the more experienced and mature. It is wonderful, as that trainer, to be surrounded by people who are:

- making eye contact

- smiling encouragingly

- leaning forward

- sitting still

- waiting expectantly for the next sentence.

Conversely, when asked to use 'closed body language' and sit as though not in the least bit interested, people respond immediately by:

- crossing arms

- turning away – or even walking away!

- avoiding eye contact

- looking bored

- fidgeting and fiddling with other things

- talking to others.

In training it is instructive to set up situations where pairs role-play scenarios in which one of them is on the receiving end of closed body language. One of the pair is given the secret instruction to act as if they are not in the least bit interested in what their partner is saying. The activity cannot run for very long because the speakers dry up and look very uncomfortable. Despite the artificial context they admit to feelings of anger, hurt, frustration and lowered self-esteem. The relationship between speaker and listener can be damaged by such listening, and even in a role-play situation, pairs need time to repair the harm. The listeners explain what they were told to do and apologise. Pairs reconvene in a circle and everyone shares their experiences of not being listened to. The litany of complaints include: doing other tasks whilst claiming to be listening, walking away, reprimanding or complaining without asking for the speaker's perspective, interrupting for incoming phone calls and cutting short the conversation because of something apparently more important. It is no wonder that, in answer to the question 'What do we need to work at our best?', the request for someone to really listen is high on everyone's agenda.

The other important point that emerges is that most people admit that they frequently listen to others in this distracted way. This self-awareness leads to a commitment to change, and in subsequent workshops participants do report that they have become more sensitive to the impact of their listening style on others.

What is at stake is not necessarily malicious intent. Many people in training admit readily that they want to give their students or their colleagues their full attention but they do not have the time. They are already required to give too much attention to too many people at one time. This is why I have chosen the term 'busy listening' rather than 'bad listening'.

Nevertheless, sensitivity to the negative impact that closed body language has on others has helped many people to make certain changes to their behaviour. They have resolved either to:

1. give full attention to those they are listening to when there is the time, or

2. recognise that there is no time at that moment and, by acknowledging the needs and the feelings of the speaker, arrange for a conversation at another time when they can concentrate and listen properly.

The latter is the '30-second empathy' conversation, accompanied by genuinely concerned body language and tone:

> *I can see that you are upset/worried/angry about something and need to talk. I am unable to give you my full attention right now because... Can we meet again at...when I can give you my full attention?*

The acknowledgement of the feelings seems to be key here, together with the message that the busy person recognises that the speaker deserves their full attention. This is not a formula set in concrete, incidentally. It is a suggestion based on the work of many teachers in role-play trying out what can help to reassure worried people, of any age, who need to talk.

An alternative response comes from the approach to personal safety promoted by the national charity Protective Behaviours UK. This programme stresses two key ideas:

1. Everyone has the right to feel safe.

2. There is nothing so big, or small, that we cannot talk about it with someone.

This approach advocates that we all have to identify and develop our own personal network of support and that we do not depend on only one person to meet our need to talk and be heard. The 30-second empathy conversation could go:

> *I can see that you are upset/worried/angry about something and need to talk. I am unable to give you my full attention right now because... Who else could you go and talk to?*

This would acknowledge that the person is feeling unsafe (in this context 'unsafe' can mean 'distressed/upset' rather than in danger, although of course this could also be the case) and that they have the right and the need to talk to someone. It also encourages people to review their support network at times of distress.

Listening with empathy

There is more to listening than using appropriate body language. It is rare that a listener sits in complete silence, only making the occasional grunt or reassuring noise. This type of complete attention is generally reserved for the counselling room or doctor's surgery. What people say in response to another can make or break a conversation. Once again the key is in the intention. There is a range of skills we can develop and practise, but the essential point is that we are trying to keep the words functioning as windows, rather than walls. Crawley (1995) gives examples of make or break responses – the types of response likely to close the conversation down include:

- judgements and 'put-downs'

- unsolicited advice – the 'shoulds', 'oughts' and 'musts'

- interrogation

- trivialising what is said

- sarcasm

- blame and accusation

- one-upmanship – 'you think you've got it bad…'

In contrast, responses that can encourage further exchange include:

- invitations to elaborate – 'tell me more…'

- acknowledgement of feeling

- appropriate facial expressions and nods

- respectful curiosity

- clarifying what the speaker needs from the listener

- checking assumptions.

Listening for feelings and needs

A key idea in the concept of Nonviolent communication, developed by Marshall Rosenberg, is that as human beings we are constantly trying to get our needs met. Sometimes we do this in inappropriate ways and sometimes we do things which have the opposite effect, largely because we have not taken the time to get in touch with what we need. Rosenberg believes that we can do this by getting in touch first with our feelings. The empathic skills listed above can create a situation in which the listener can help the speaker to get in touch with what is going on inside – their feelings, their stories, their needs, and the confidence in their own ability to find ways forward. It provides some extra strategies for teasing out the elements of Figure 3.1, referred to earlier.

The writers of an excellent book on listening to young people (Faber and Mazlish 1980) give examples of various listening styles that can close people down, including belittling or ignoring feelings, giving unwanted advice, asking too many questions, and being over-sympathetic to the point of pity, and sum up:

> But let someone really listen, let someone acknowledge my inner pain and give me a chance to talk more about what's troubling me and I begin to feel less upset, less confused, more able to cope with my feelings and problems. (p.8)

Most of our day-to-day conversations do not require us to put on our empathic listening hat, practise restraint and give a special space to the other person. 'Normal' conversation is about the equal give and take of such skills. However, our antennae need to be out for when this is required, and there is no harm in being empathic even in the tiny conversations we have with people we meet throughout the day. Greeting people by name, asking how people are, and being interested in the response; all these help everyone feel valued and cared for. This behaviour, encouraged and developed amongst young people in class groups, plants the seeds of community and creates an inclusive atmosphere. In staff rooms and corridors, modelled by the senior management to colleagues and students, this practice can transform the atmosphere. A listening school will feel warm and welcoming, so that when someone really needs to talk they know there will be someone there ready and able to listen.

Reviewing and modelling good practice

Initial teacher training rarely includes training in empathic listening skills. Once teachers are in post there is little opportunity for constructive feedback on whether they are good listeners. It is ironic that a common complaint made by teachers is that young people do not listen, and yet the young people themselves complain that teachers do not listen to them. Clearly here is an issue that needs addressing.

The decision to review listening skills and opportunities throughout the school provides the excuse for colleagues to support each other by giving constructive feedback. After all, these skills are fundamental to developing good relationships in the classroom and the staff room. Furthermore it is vital that staff are modelling these skills in their day-to-day interactions with young people. This modelling is more important than lessons dedicated to teaching such skills. As is often said, young people learn from what adults do, not what we say should be done. If we want to be listened to, we need to set a good example ourselves.

I remember introducing circle time into a school when I was still teaching but did not have a regular tutor group of my own that year. More is said about circle time in Chapter 7. Suffice it to say here that it is a process that allows for the development of many restorative and relational skills including empathic listening. I ran circle time across the Year 7 tutor groups during their timetabled tutorial slot, taking about six weeks with each group. The tutor of each group participated in the circle, taking part in every activity as an equal participant. In every tutor group, bar one, the tutors could see that the respect and empathy generated in the circle was something they wanted to take into their day-to-day interactions with their groups. The students in these tutor groups started to use the skills amongst themselves, and the atmosphere in these groups was supportive and warm.

The exception was a group in which, as soon as the bell went, and the circle time session ended, the tutor took back the reins from me and used the last few minutes to harangue and nag her group about a current concern. She even admitted, in their hearing, that she was not using the skills we had been developing. The message was loud and clear to her students. As far as their tutor was concerned, the skills we had been using with each other were only for circle time. Not surprisingly perhaps, this tutor group had the most behavioural problems that year.

Restorative enquiry

What follows is a structure inspired by the model of restorative conferencing promoted by the Thames Valley Police (2001). It uses all of the elements of the empathetic listening already described; the technique is recommended for any situation when the listener needs to remain impartial so as to create a space for the speaker to reflect on what has happened and identify a way forward.

Take a look back at Figure 3.1. It illustrates the way in which what we think, the way we feel, what we need and what we do are all interrelated. Key questions, as outlined in Tables 3.1 and 3.2, can enable speakers to tell their story effectively.

The rationale behind the process is that, first, the enquirer is inviting reflection on the past, then on the present and finally on what needs to happen in the future. By adhering to the structure the listener limits their own input and ensures that the enquiry does not become skewed to their own agenda, whatever that may be. It also puts equal emphasis on the elements of behaviour, thoughts, feelings and needs.

Table 3.1 Restorative enquiry: The past	
Suggested question	*Focus*
Can you explain what happened?	thinking (interpretation) and behaviour
What were you thinking at the time?	thinking
How were you feeling at the time?	feelings
Who else do you think has been affected by this?	others' feelings, thoughts and behaviours

Table 3.2 Restorative enquiry: The present and future	
Suggested question	*Focus*
What have been your thoughts since? What are they now?	thinking
How are you feeling now?	feelings
What do you need (to do) so that: • things can be put right? • the harm can be repaired? • you can move on? (This question can be adapted to suit the context.)	needs

Opportunities for debriefing using restorative enquiry need to be part of the management of challenging situations. Staff burnout owing to the continued stress of managing conflict might be halted if people were helped to develop these skills when such challenges have occurred. The Chinese written character for 'conflict' incorporates the concepts of both 'crisis' and 'opportunity'. The restorative school uses all conflicts as opportunities for everyone involved to learn and do things differently next time, adults and young people alike. Examples in a school setting include:

- Discussion between a teacher and a student following an incident that has caused concern to either person. In a restorative school this would replace the more prevalent approach of a 'telling off' following what is sometimes called 'disruptive behaviour', usually attributed to the young person alone. The approach may allow the meanings behind the behaviour to be expressed.

- Discussion between a member of the school staff and another colleague, to help the former reflect on any situation that has caused them concern. This opportunity can also be called a restorative debriefing and is sadly not often available to school staff in the aftermath of challenging situations. Failure to provide non-judgemental support and opportunities for reflection and development can lead to staff absenteeism and burnout, especially amongst the teaching staff (Brouwers and Tomic 2000).

- Preparatory meetings for a restorative intervention involving two or more people when there has been harm caused or conflict has occurred. (These interventions are described in later chapters.)

- Discussions between school staff and parents.

The restorative enquiry model is adaptable to many contexts and only a few are suggested here. It relates closely to the restorative interventions that will be described in later chapters amd the model used to illustrate the process will be a recurring theme. It is helpful to see restorative processes developing from some key ideas, skills and concepts. The model can serve as a simple aide-memoire for restorative practitioners on a day-to-day basis. It is also simple enough to use as the basis for work with young people on emotional literacy, relationship development and conflict-solving skills.

Restorative conversations – Building, maintaining and repairing relationships

The essential skills of open body language and empathic responses can be used on a daily basis with students and colleagues. Even without organisational changes, such skills, developed and used across the school community, can contribute to a warmer, more supportive environment. For some people these are second nature. For others they need developing, practising and reviewing constantly.

A school community is a complex social web, and certain actions in one place can have a knock-on effect somewhere else. Giving people time, attention and empathy can boost their confidence and their ability to provide these for someone else. In time, the positive interactions between the whole community become second nature, but at first it takes conscious effort.

If the school climate is a hostile one then it might feel like an uphill struggle to turn things around. However, it can be reassuring to know that small changes by a few people can begin to make a difference.

> Never doubt that a small group of thoughtful, committed citizens can change the world: indeed, it's the only thing that ever has.
>
> Margaret Mead (1901–1978)

Restorative listening skills – Who has them?

There are many opportunities for people in a school community to the empathic listening skills, and many opportunities lost. Part of the review whether or not a school is indeed a 'listening school' would include a review of where such discussions could be improved and what, structurally, needs to be in place for them to happen.

There are undoubtedly many situations in a school day where what is required is the kind of active non-judgemental listening described in the chapter, but what actually happens is very different. It might be necessary to invite everyone, in the early stages of change, to be very self-reflective in their day-to-day interactions with each other.

It almost goes without saying that the key to whole school change is the example set by the senior management team and, most importantly, the headteacher. More will be said in subsequent chapters about running meetings along restorative lines, but even at the basic level of empathic listening it is vital that the senior management team is giving the lead.

A self-appraisal of their current skill level might be useful at the outset to ensure that they are able to model good practice. This is good restorative practice and good leadership. The senior management are demonstrating that they are prepared to do what they are asking everyone else to do – review their own practice and make changes where necessary.

The following questions are suggested for self-review (see Appendix C for a photocopiable questionnaire). If the team feels safe and there is sufficient trust it could be done with peer feedback.

- Am I approachable?

- Do people feel safe to talk to me about their concerns?

- Do I ensure that there are no interruptions wherever possible?

- Do I appear interested in what people are saying?

- Do I listen in a respectful way?

- Do I acknowledge their feelings?

- Do I let people finish what they need to say before I respond?

- Do I check with people what kind of response they need from me?

- Do I respect people's views even when I don't agree with them?

- After talking to me do people feel heard?

- How do I know the answers to all of the above?

- Have I asked people, or am I making assumptions?

...ires can be developed for each 'constituency' of the school. ...ffice staff and catering staff each have their own particular ...iderations and some of the questions might depend on a person's ...nool. In drawing up the questions it is probably useful to consider ...ctions each group has during a school day and what skills make for ...effective outcome. In this way people can review what they do, how ...o it and thus identify any specific further training.

...Appendix C includes examples of some of the issues other groups may want ...onsider, in addition to relevant questions from the list above.

Children and young people

Young people need to learn a variety of different types of listening. It is important to differentiate between listening for information and listening in the context of relationship building. There is a skill in critically listening and learning from someone with whom one is not in relationship at that moment. Examples of this would include listening to the radio, the television, a public speaker, a college lecturer or a teacher in front of a class. Many such skills are highlighted in the National Curriculum and the teaching of them is given some attention at teacher training college.

There is undoubtedly a need to develop listening for learning, but this is not what is meant in the current chapter. What is at stake here is the skills needed to connect with another human being. The confusion between listening for information and listening actively and empathically can result in conflict and misunderstanding. Many adults confuse the two. We need to ensure that young people recognise the difference.

A listening school would create opportunities for young people to use their speaking and listening skills with each other in ways that build the sense of belonging and community. In this way the Standards Agenda, with its concentration on academic targets, would overlap with the Inclusion Agenda, which fosters belonging, community and a collective responsibility to care and support each other. Later chapters consider relational and restorative processes such as circle time, peer mediation, peer mentoring, buddying schemes and school councils. All of these provide opportunities for listening skills to be developed.

Case study – Negotiating ground rules

My Year 9 bottom-set French group was not the easiest of classes to teach. Despite what I thought were interesting, lively, lessons, learning French was not top of their priorities. Discussions about what they had seen on the telly the night before, or who had said what to whom during the break, were of far more interest. It would have been lovely if such conversations were had in French, and indeed I would have encouraged them, but unfortunately this was a bridge too far.

I felt we needed to take stock and so, quite early in the school year, I called a halt to the *bain de français* that was de rigeur for the time (i.e. running the lesson entirely in the target language) and, sitting in a circle, invited the class to identify their rights as far as learning was concerned. Slightly startled to be invited to have such a discussion, the young people were all keen to list these, and told me it was the first time anyone had asked them such a question.

What was slightly more challenging was the next question. If they had certain rights, what were their responsibilities towards each other to ensure that everyone had their rights honoured? Hence a right to be listened to entailed a responsibility to allow everyone to have their say and be heard. The right to learn at their own pace entailed a responsibility to let others learn at theirs, without disruptions.

Gradually a sense of shared responsibility for the good running of the lessons was developed in the group. I accepted responsibility for preparing interesting, accessible lessons and they acknowledged their own role in participating and helping each other.

If things did not go to plan, and I felt unhappy or irritated, I would stop the class and ask how everyone else was feeling, and what they wanted to do to get back on course. Technically speaking they all had the right to do this, but since I was the only teacher using this approach I understood how the students did not feel comfortable with it.

Lessons did not always go smoothly, but we did have some fun and the students did learn a lot more French than they would have done. They also learnt a lot about each other, the impact of their behaviour on each other and their responsibilities as students.

Summary

This chapter has focused on developing the 'listening school'. It describes essential listening skills that enable at least one person in a conversation to hear the feelings and needs of the other, even if these are not expressed overtly. It has used the phrase 'restorative listening' to characterise this behaviour, and identified it as a fundamental building block in a whole school restorative approach. It has also described a restorative tool called 'restorative enquiry', which can help any member of the school community receive support after a challenging situation and learn from it. Finally it has highlighted the importance of restorative listening becoming common currency throughout a school community and has suggested ways of identifying where there needs to be training and support.

Listening to others' feelings and needs is one side of a restorative conversation. Articulating them in a way that gets heard, particularly in challenging situations, is the other. This is the focus of the next chapter.

Chapter 4

Restorative Conversation – Talking the Talk

> Restorative justice to me is the way forward for all schools; it gives all parties the right to be listened to, and to feel they have been heard.
>
> Primary Learning Support Assistant

Active and empathic listening can be relatively easy if the people in conversation are not in direct conflict with each other or are not having a challenging and potentially difficult conversation. The stakes are raised, however, if what is being said can be interpreted as a threat or an attack, or would appear to contradict the experience of the other person. Conflicts of interest and an imbalance of power can both start to play a part in what can rapidly escalate into a hostile exchange. This chapter considers the restorative skills and approaches needed when two people broach a potentially difficult conversation or find themselves in conflict unexpectedly. It also describes some of the techniques that can be used in a training workshop to allow people to develop their restorative conversation skills and receive supportive feedback.

Winning the argument – Do we need to?

It is a novel concept for some people that a discussion involving disagreement need not be a battle in which someone wins and someone loses. The metaphors we use in English for discussion tend to emphasise the conflictual side of dialogue (Lakoff and Johnson 1980). We talk about taking sides, winning or losing an argument, attacking someone's position, defending a point of view, feeling defeated or triumphant, and so on. Many people are brought up to think that if they have a different perspective from someone else the task is to win this person over, persuade or convince – rather than simply to be curious about the differences.

Even when there is an attempt to find some middle ground we use an expression that has an implication of something that is less than ideal – a compromise. The word can also mean to give up on some of one's beliefs or needs, to give way and concede ground – another battle metaphor.

The concept of the 'win-win' solution is potentially radical (Cornelius and Faire 1993), but it is the ideal outcome of a difference in opinion or perspective – a way forward with which everyone is satisfied and ideally has their needs met. It is the ideal outcome from any restorative process, and the intention of working towards it needs to underpin restorative discussion.

It takes time to listen properly to someone, to be listened to as well, and to hear about and acknowledge each other's perspective, feelings and needs in a given situation. This is undeniable. However, the alternative is not a quick fix. The alternative, where one person imposes a solution and others concede, can lead to resentments and hostility that bristle beneath the surface and eventually contaminate a working or personal relationship. Postponing a difficult conversation is understandable, but in the long run probably more damaging and painful than preparing for, and having, it.

Having difficult conversations

Conversations can be difficult for many different reasons, and we instinctively shy away from them unless we enjoy conflict – and some people do. It is interesting to note that in preparation for learning the skills of a mediator, trainees who are asked to freely associate with the word 'conflict' rarely mention positive words. It is unusual for someone to suggest words such as 'change', 'dynamic' and 'energy'. Nevertheless, a lively, thoughtful family, group or team that never found themselves in conflict or disagreement would be a very unusual one. The manual produced by the organisation LEAP, *Playing with Fire* (Fine and Macbeth 1992), uses the metaphor of the fire to illustrate the different potentials of conflict. In both scenarios the fuel is people. The spark can be a sense of dissatisfaction, injustice, concern or outrage. What happens next is crucial. The spark can begin a process of smouldering. On the one hand this can mean people talking together, sharing their sense of injustice, galvanising people to action and gathering strength. On the other this smouldering could mean rumours being spread and cliques forming, one against another.

The fire catches alight when these groups begin to take action. Conversations in private are more openly expressed. Seen in a positive light this might mean public meetings and a campaign of awareness-raising. The negative side would be fostering hatred and gathering arms. The full-scale conflagration might mean a revolution for change or a war. One route could lead to a better society, the other to pain, suffering and death. Opportunity on the one hand, crisis on the other – to recall the Chinese written character for conflict, mentioned in Chapter 3.

On a smaller, less dramatic, scale, conflicts in school can also take different routes. Dissatisfaction with aspects of the school policy can lead to difficult conversations, and possibly conflicts between all sorts of different constituencies within the school. A restorative school will try and adopt a restorative approach to deal with these conflicts, and ensure people in the school community have the skills to engage in this way. This approach will not always result in win-win solutions. Human beings are not perfect and the best conflict-management skills can be abandoned in the heat of the moment. However, the will can be there, and if things go wrong then there is always an opportunity for debriefing, using the skills of restorative enquiry described in the previous chapter.

Different perspectives, feelings and needs

Conversations can be difficult when people see things very differently. Curiously enough, if we accept that we all see things differently this is not a threatening idea (Stone *et al.* 1999). There is no one 'true' version of events when more than one person is involved in a situation, since we all make sense of our experience in different ways, as the poem about the Six Blind Men and the Elephant reminds us (see Chapter 3). This is what makes our interactions endlessly fascinating, and also potentially tricky.

All restorative processes stress the importance of recognising that we all have different perspectives, but also that we often have common needs. Resolution of conflict can result from acknowledging the differences and finding the common ground.

Later in the chapter I describe some of the training techniques that can be used to help people develop their conflict-management skills. What follows here is a brief description of the essential elements and a suggested structure. It is inspired by the same model I used in the previous chapter to describe restorative enquiry, and this is not surprising. A restorative conversation will be one in which both sides are using restorative enquiry techniques.

It may be useful at this point to consider two people facing each other, each with their interacting thoughts, feelings, needs and behaviours (see Figure 4.1 on the next page.)

When Person A says or does something – which is a behaviour – Person B sees or hears something (also a behaviour). This then triggers thoughts and feelings in Person B, as they interpret and respond emotionally. They may, in turn, say or do something in response (more behaviour).

Much of the time the interactions between people happen so quickly that they may believe they are not choosing what they think, feel or do. In fact there is scope to change any of these elements if people stay in touch with what is going on inside them. Our interpretation of events can lead us to feel certain things and behave in certain ways. Taking a step back and considering whether this event has a different possible interpretation can sometimes change the feelings and thus the subsequent behaviour.

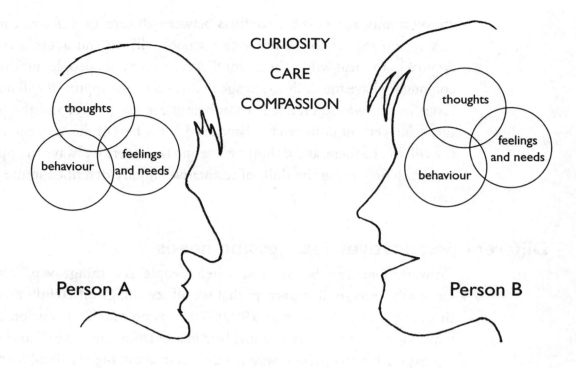

Figure 4.1 Curiosity, care and compassion – the keys to resolving conflict.

In potentially challenging situations asking questions about other people's interpretations of behaviour, their feelings and their needs can help give that opportunity to review and reflect, see things differently and thus possibly feel and act differently.

For those meeting these ideas for the first time it can be useful to have recourse to a structure or formula for the process described above. Many people are familiar with 'I' messages, for example. These are statements that encourage us to take ownership of our feelings, rather than use the blaming approach that starts:

You make me (mad/furious, etc.) *when you…*

This kind of accusation is generally spoken in a hostile tone, often with accusatory body language, such as a pointed finger. An 'I' message, on the other hand, begins with the speaker acknowledging their own feelings, and possibly that the problem is their own (AVP 1986; Crawley 1995; Fine and Macbeth 1992; Rosenberg 1999). One begins by owning the problem:

I have a problem I'd like to discuss.

before continuing

When I see/hear… (followed by a description phrased as neutrally as possible)

I feel…

What I need is…

So would you be willing to…?

The approach is a very useful one in preparing for a difficult conversation. Marshall Rosenberg adds a helpful twist for interpreting others' unrestorative outbursts (Rosenberg 1999). In such circumstances he suggests turning the formula around:

So when you see/hear…

Are you perhaps feeling…?

Do you need…?

And would you like…?

I have been very inspired by these ideas, which build on similar formulas I have found in other conflict management and mediation manuals and have used with success in my own personal and professional life.

Whilst Nonviolent communication puts emphasis on the feelings and needs of people in conflict, other conflict-management styles encourage a sharing of viewpoints, in the belief that these are bound to be different and that the key to understanding is curiosity (Crawley 1995; Stone *et al.* 1999).

Returning to the restorative enquiry model, it is clear that this is an approach that brings in all three of the circles – thinking (which includes the story we tell ourselves about our own and others' behaviour), feelings and needs. During a potentially difficult conversation the two speakers need to be in touch with their own thoughts, feelings, needs and actions, and also curious about those of the other person. It will be a matter of judgement when to articulate aspects of one's own 'interlocking circles' and when to enquire about the other person's. Time for silent reflection and taking stock will be vital in such an exchange.

In my experience such formulas are most helpful when considered more as guidelines and underlying principles, rather than as scripts that need to be adhered to. Some practitioners advocate that they be used more in the preparation for a difficult conversation. I have found the principles useful to keep in mind as a conversation develops, even if the phrases I use differ from what is described above.

Referring back to the restorative conversation structure (Figure 4.1), what follows are some suggested guidelines. They are written from the viewpoint of one of the speakers (Person A), someone versed in restorative approaches:

Person A – *So tell me what happened / what is going on from your perspective?*

Person B – (replies with their interpretation)

Person A – *So let me just check I have got this right – you are saying that...*

This is a useful skill – reflecting back one's understanding of what has been said to demonstrate attentive listening, empathy and respect for the story. Next there is a judgement call – is the other person ready and able to listen to Person A's perspective without closing down, going on the defensive or even the attack? If they are then the next step might be:

Person A – *Can I tell you what happened / what is going on from my perspective?*

If Person B is not ready to hear an alternative perspective then Person A may need to go through the restorative enquiry questions all at once and hope that at the end the speaker will feel able to offer them similar attention and restraint.

Alternatively Person A might be able to suggest alternating exchanges by commenting about what is going on. This could be done all at once, or by Person A guiding the interchange:

Person A – *Why don't we both explain how we see things, how we feel about it all and then what we both need to put things right? Maybe then we can find a way forward we can both agree on?*

Or, in stages:

Person A – *How do you see things?*

Person B – (Explains)

Person A – *So what you are saying is... Now, let me tell you how I see it... Do you mind telling me what you have heard me say so I can check I've explained myself clearly?*

(followed by a similar process for feelings and needs)

The guiding principle throughout the exchange is ensuring that both sides express their interlocking circles of perspective (thinking), feelings and needs, and acknowledge they have heard those of the other person.

Expressing needs is one thing, and getting them met is another. Marshall Rosenberg cautions against expecting that just because we tell someone our needs they are automatically obliged to meet them. However, identifying our needs can help us then sort out how to meet them ourselves or in a different way.

The type of exchange described above sounds rather unnatural written down. The knack is to incorporate the essence of it into our own natural everyday language and to use the ideas and aims behind it to prepare ourselves for a potentially difficult conversation. The words are definitely not a formula or a script and I have used them simply as a way of trying to exemplify what could be said at each stage.

Developing restorative discussion skills

People have a lot of natural and instinctive understanding about what to do in difficult situations, and what follows are ways to tap this knowledge and bring it to the surface. This approach to training is congruent with the restorative philosophy that those with a problem are the best people to resolve it.

I want to acknowledge that my sources of inspiration for this style of training come from my experience working with LEAP – Confronting Conflict, the Alternatives to Violence Project and Mediation UK's experiential training approach. Details of all these organisations are to be found in the list of useful contacts at the end of the book. Over the years I have used and adapted many of the activities first found during my involvement with these and other organisations. I like to think we can share and adapt ideas, sometimes forgetting the original source, but acknowledging some of the inspiration.

Starting points – Circle work on conflict

The group sits in a circle and begins the session with some ice-breakers and warm-ups to get acquainted and feel as safe as possible with each other. This takes time and cannot be forced or rushed.

Planning work on dealing with conflict needs care, and safety is a key issue. I suggest beginning with light-hearted, unthreatening activities before embarking on what is described here. I would also intersperse challenging activities with these light-hearted activities to release tension, have a laugh, change the dynamic when needed and allow people to take stock. In the Alternatives to Violence Project, working with inmates in prisons and young offenders' institutions, these activities are called 'Light and Livelies' and are a vital part of an intensive three-day programme.

When the group seems ready, I invite suggestions about the sorts of conflicts they have to deal with. Depending on the group this might be challenging situations with or between students, with parents, with colleagues, in staff meetings or with behaviour support agency staff. The choice of case study is a matter of judgement, but I would tend to err on the side of using what is most alive for the group. To avoid the real conflicts people are facing during a course on conflict management does not give a good message.

Having listed a few options and decided which one to use, it is time to put some life into the two disputants (group conflicts can be addressed at a later stage).

At this point the facts of the case can be relaxed slightly so as to create a more generic, and potentially more widely useful, scenario. For example, if the original situation was between a teacher and a student, participants are invited to invent a personality for the teacher and for the student and these can be written up on a flipchart or board. This can be quite a cathartic experience and can help people express fears and needs, share problems and laugh at themselves.

Once the characters have been brought to life, with a name, an age, character traits and a bit more background to the situation, volunteers are invited to play the roles. This may take some persuasion but if more light-hearted activities have preceded this then usually people feel safe enough to give it a go.

There are certain guidelines that need to be in place:

1. Volunteers can freeze the action at any point and stop, or ask for help.

2. Anyone taking a role needs to know that they will be formally de-roled at the end of the process. It is useful to start with a fairly unthreatening example so that people can see the de-role process for themselves early on.

3. Although what is learned can be shared outside of the circle, what is said in the circle stays there unless express permission is given otherwise.

4. Anyone in a role wears a sticky label with their assumed name written on it, and whilst they are wearing this label they are in role. It is important to consider this when asking them to put on the label and when de-roling.

De-roling is a vital part of the experiential training style used here, and failure to do it thoroughly can leave people stranded in role and very vulnerable. The process involves participants in the role-play being invited to comment on how they are feeling in the role before reverting back to their normal selves. This is usually done by taking off the sticky label bearing their role name, sticking it on their chair, moving to a different chair and giving a word of advice to their character. The facilitator then throws the sticky label away and invites the role-player to explain one way in which they differ from the character they were playing. Scenarios can be exploited for their learning potential in a variety of different ways. I describe three of my favourites here:

- 'Fishbowl'

- 'Hot seating'

- 'Coaching'.

These seem to be terms used commonly in a lot of training in this vein.

FISHBOWL

In this technique the two volunteers begin their conversation in the circle, watched by everyone else who is sitting around. The action can be frozen at any time either by the facilitator or by the volunteers and people have a chance to comment on what they see happening. Advice can be given from the circle, although the volunteers are free to ignore the advice if they prefer. As ever, it is important to emphasise that everyone is seeing the situation through their own filter, and their opinions and advice reflect their own interpretation, feelings and needs at the time. The action is then unfrozen. It can either be rewound and the situation dealt with differently, or taken up from the point it left off.

The technique can be used to give volunteers an opportunity to try out a new strategy and observers can give feedback and advice on how best to use the strategies. Many new strategies will come from the participants themselves and grow out of the activity. Ideas for developing particular aspects are also described later.

HOT SEATING

In this technique two volunteers begin the conversation and at a given point the action can be frozen by the facilitator, by a role-player or even by an observer. At this point someone from the circle swaps with the role-player to try out an idea they may have in order to advance the situation. If the scenario is halted by an observer it would usually be because this person saw an opportunity for trying out something new, and it would be this person who moves into the circle.

In this technique it is unlikely that a role-player will get too deeply into role but the facilitator needs to be alert to the need for sensitive de-roling at the end.

COACHING

In this technique the two volunteers have two coaches close by, ready to give them advice and support when the action is frozen. It can be useful to give these coaches a specific role. One option is to invite one of the coaches for each 'adversary' to coach them on expressing feelings and the other to coach them on articulating needs. Another option is to ask the coaches to advise on expressing feelings and thoughts.

I usually set up the scene in the middle of the circle, inviting the role-players to sit, stand, move or keep still, depending on the context. The coaches sit or stand behind the person they are supporting, and the role-player turns to them for ideas when the action is frozen (see Figure 4.2). (This is a variant on an activity called 'The Boxing Ring' used by LEAP – Confronting Conflict. I have found the inspiration of this organisation invaluable.)

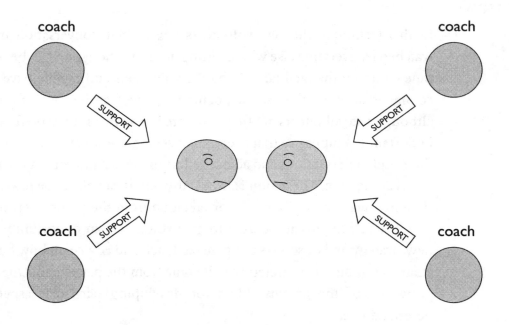

Figure 4.2 Role-play technique using coaches to help volunteers express themselves

Often coaches need support too, since these can be new concepts and in any case teasing out separate strands of feelings, needs and thoughts is tricky as they are inevitably interwoven. This supporting task is the role of the wider circle.

The skills of the facilitator are required to balance the theoretical discussions of the coaches with the energy and immediacy of the role-play itself. Too much talking *about* the scene can get in the way of the experience itself. Experiential training emphasises that people learn from having the actual experience. Role-play is used to approximate as closely as possible to a real life experience, but in a safe and supportive environment.

Ideas for the skills practice circle

YOUR TURN, MY TURN

A simple technique taught to very young children, mentioned in the excellent set of conflict resolution materials for Key Stage 1–3 *Playground Peacemakers* (Farrington 2000), is 'Your turn, my turn', in which children as young as five and six are taught to recognise potentially difficult situations, stop themselves, recognise they are about to fall out and invite their potential adversary to tell their story first and say how they are feeling and then tell their own side. It is a simple technique and one that adults could benefit from using too. This could be the starting point for working with conflict. Beginning by listening to the other person's point of view can be novel for some.

The conversation could start naturally and, at the point when things escalate, one person can stop and acknowledge what is happening, and invite the other to have their say first. Young people can be guided by semi-scripted suggestions along the lines of:

> *Let's not fall out over this. Why don't you tell me how you see it and then I'll do the same. I'm sure we can sort this out.*

This is a simple first step, already described earlier in the chapter.

Expressing and acknowledging strong emotions

Feelings are at the heart of difficult conversations – that is why they are difficult. Avoiding feelings will only make matters worse. They will leak out in what we say, how we say it and our deafening body language. When we have difficulties in expressing our feelings we sometimes pull away from people and become distant.

We can be afraid of expressing strong emotion for fear of the consequences. We fear losing control, becoming destructive in our anger and making matters worse. However, in the long term unexpressed negative emotion can make matters worse anyway by causing illness, stress and bad atmospheres.

We are brought up to believe that certain feelings are best not expressed. Typically, for example, men are brought up not to admit and show feelings of distress or inability to cope. However, all families have their own 'tradition' of what to do, or not do, with certain emotions. How many people were taught as children how to deal creatively with anger, for example? For many people feeling angry and acting angrily are synonymous, so the only two choices are suppressing the feelings or lashing out. Doing something different from this tradition can be challenging – and scary! The following activity can help people understand what might be behind their own and another's anger. It was inspired by an idea from the LEAP manual *Playing with Fire*. The role-playing aspect of the activity is preceded by some personal reflection on an angry situation. Participants are invited to complete, in private and on paper, the sentence:

> *I felt angry when...*

The facilitator draws a large onion on the flipchart with the word 'Anger' on the top layer of the onion skin (see Figure 4.3). The facilitator then invites completion of the following sentences (explaining that the focus is the same incident each time) and writes the highlighted new word on the appropriate layer of the onion:

> *I felt hurt because...*
>
> *What I needed was...*
>
> *My fear was that...*

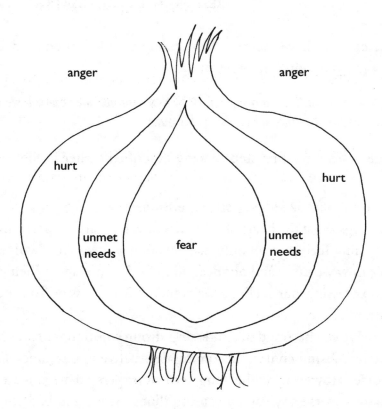

Figure 4.3 The 'Anger Onion' with its layers of underlying emotions

On completion of the activity participants can share their sentences with a partner if they want to. Sometimes another person can help us see what the underlying emotions were, even when we fail to see them ourselves.

The role-play stage of this activity might revolve around people identifying a situation in which they feel or have felt angry. Using one of the three skills practice techniques (Fishbowl, Hot seating or Coaching), role-players receive suggestions from others on how to express what is beneath the surface in a way that gets their needs met, if possible. Failing this, the exercise may at least help role-players see what their unmet needs are, and give food for thought about where or how they can be met or, at worst, lived with.

The 'interlocking circles' idea underpinning restorative enquiry and restorative conversation can be used to inform the support being given. However, it is important to acknowledge that many people already have their own personal set of strategies. Restorative training builds on this natural wisdom. To discount anything that does not fit into the proposed restorative model would be disempowering and disrespectful. The point is to ensure that strategies are respectful, empathic and address everyone's feelings and needs.

As a final note I usually stress that it is risky to think other people's feelings are more important than our own. If we ignore our own feelings then others will too – to the detriment of any meaningful relationship.

Identity issues

According to Stone and his colleagues at the Harvard Negotiation Project (Stone *et al.* 1999), there are three key elements to our sense of identity, underpinned by three needs:

1. Our sense of self-worth is underpinned by our need to feel like a worthwhile and essentially good person and considered so by others.

2. We also need to belong and to feel liked and likeable, if not even lovable.

3. Our self-confidence depends on needing to feel competent at what we do and be judged by others to be so.

Conversations can feel difficult if we sense that any one of the three aspects of our identity is being criticised. In fact if we are criticised, or feel criticised, about any of these issues it is possible that we will experience what Stone *et al.* describe as an 'Identity Quake'. Our reactions may not be rational and balanced as a result.

Preparing for knocks to our identity is challenging because they can take us unawares. Some preparation in terms of accepting ourselves, and not being defined by others' judgements, can help. So can avoiding setting ourselves too high a standard, so that a criticism of our competence in one area does not then mean we tell ourselves we are totally incompetent in everything we do. One useful message that my father once gave me might be: 'Our weaknesses are our strengths taken to excess!'

It can also help to recognise our sensitive areas and notice when conversations throw us off balance. Finally we need to remember that it is all right to make mistakes; our own intentions and motivations are likely to be complex and we may well have contributed to a problem. We need to be open.

In training it can be interesting to use the coaching technique and give the two role-players three coaches who have had time to consider the importance of

1. respecting the other's story

2. expressing one's feelings and acknowledging the other person's

3. potential identity quakes.

Another variant is to divide the observers into three different groups and ask each group to provide suggestions and support in each of these three areas. Whenever the role-play is frozen, coaches or coaching teams can comment on whether the role-player might benefit from articulating more explicitly what is going on inside their head.

Restorative conversations in school

In the previous chapter I identified situations that might call for the skills and technique of restorative enquiry. The opportunities for restorative conversations are much wider. One-sided conversations, in which one person talks and the other person just listens, or uses questions to draw out the speaker's perspective without giving their own, are perhaps less common. (In fact these skills are precisely what are required for the restorative interventions of mediation and restorative conferences, which will be described in later chapters.)

Opportunities for restorative conversation occur daily, whenever two people engage in a conversation that goes beyond simple greetings or exchange of factual information. They come into their own however in situations such as:

- after incidents in a classroom when two people disagree about what was appropriate behaviour, and have perhaps exchanged damaging remarks

- when a teacher and a parent or carer need to discuss a young person and share their different perspectives on a situation

- when colleagues need to air a grievance between each other.

A restorative school would ensure that in such situations restorative conversations become the norm and are highlighted in the relevant policies regarding relationship management, home–school protocols and internal grievance procedures. Since the skills and the approach may be new to many staff initially, it is recommended that opportunities be given for the type of skills practice described earlier in the chapter, with supportive and constructively critical feedback. Debriefing with peers, using the restorative enquiry technique, could also help members of the school community reflect on their practice. Peer mentors or buddies could play a part in this transitional stage, both for students and adults. Everyone is thereby encouraged to be reflective restorative practitioners.

Case study – Emphatic listening

I was running a short course on conflict management for the residents of a residential home together with a colleague. It was the second week and they were gathering in the sitting room ready to begin our session. It was not obligatory, but we tried to create a relaxed, informal atmosphere so we could address the many issues of conflict that seemed to be part of the everyday lives of these young people.

I was standing in the corridor when Sharon came hurtling down the stairs, dressed up to the nines, ready to go out. One of the residential staff reminded her that our session was about to commence.

'******', she replied angrily. 'I'm not going to no ****** session. I'm off out.'

Since she had not attended the first session I had not met Sharon before. I smiled and said hello, and quietly acknowledged that she seemed very angry, and asked if it was because she felt she was obliged to come to our session. I assured her it was voluntary. Indeed I do not even remember trying to persuade her to come.

I don't think her anger had anything to do with me, nor was her swearing aimed at me. In fact as soon as I had greeted her in a friendly way, acknowledged that she was angry and shown I was trying to understand why she might be so angry, she changed completely – like a hot air balloon that had just been deflated.

'Well, alright then – I'll come for just half an hour,' she growled, much to my surprise and delight. And she did, for half an hour…which was, after all, what she had promised.

Summary

This chapter has developed the skills of restorative enquiry and described how they can be adapted to the needs of two people faced with a potentially difficult exchange. It refers to the process described as restorative conversation and advocates the approach as a set of guidelines rather than a formula.

Examples of training techniques are given and those beginning to use restorative approaches in their daily exchanges are recommended to practise the skills initially in supportive groups. Ongoing support from peers is also recommended using mentors or buddies.

The skills of restorative enquiry and restorative conversation are the foundations of the next stage – facilitating other people's conflicts or grievances. The progression from interpersonal skills to the facilitator skills described in the following chapters is based on the belief that, as restorative practitioners, we first need to learn how to help ourselves through difficult or harmful situations if we are going to offer to help others do the same. That is not to say that restorative practitioners never need the support of others. Indeed there are times when, for all sorts of reasons, we are unable, or choose not, to be our own facilitators. However, the point is still a valid one. Restorative practitioners need to 'walk the walk' and 'talk the talk', and this will be what transforms a school, a community and, eventually, society at large.

Chapter 5
Repairing Harm Through Mediation

Restorative justice provides the opportunity for both parties to feel comfortable and leave the situation empowered.

Year Head, Secondary School

This chapter describes a process of mediation that can be used in schools between people of all ages. It relates the skills needed to facilitate this process to those already described in previous chapters and discusses what other skills are needed. It also highlights the potential differences between mediating between people in conflict and mediating when harm has been caused (and responsibility for this harm acknowledged) by at least one of the people in the process. In the world beyond the school gates the former is often used in neighbourhood disputes by community mediation services and the latter by services supporting victims and offenders. In my experience these differences are often blurred in school, and responsibility can shift as the plot thickens and more is revealed.

The chapter suggests opportunities for using mediation in the school context and also refers to real examples of how mediation is currently being used in schools in the UK.

Training issues are considered at the end of the chapter, relating these to what has already been described in earlier chapters.

What is mediation?

Mediation is a process in which people in conflict are supported by a neutral third party (or parties) to hear each other's story and find a mutually acceptable way forward. It gives people the opportunity to appreciate the impact of their behaviour on other people, whether this behaviour was wilfully harmful or inadvertently so. Peer mediation is the term given to this process when the mediators are young people mediating their peers. A key principle of mediation is that the people with the conflict are the ones best placed to find ways forward. Imposed solutions do not necessarily address the underlying resentment and bitterness which conflict can cause. Mediation provides an opportunity for exploring these and repairing the harm done to relationships caused by conflict.

There are a variety of different mediation styles being used around the world (see Boserup 2002). The style I use, and train others to use, is constantly evolving as I learn more and read about new approaches. I also believe that we tend to adopt a personal approach, blending our own personalities with our life and professional experiences. Nevertheless, I also believe that to be restorative the mediation style we use must be as empowering as possible and must essentially belong to those in the conflict or dispute.

My current inspirations include the transformative mediation style of Bush and Folger (Bush and Folger 1994) and the narrative approach of Cloke and Goldsmith that recognises the power of storytelling (Cloke and Goldsmith 2000). The transformative style places emphasis on opportunities for empowering those in a conflict, on the grounds that conflict can be a very disempowering, confusing, disabling state to be in. It also acknowledges that in conflict we can sometimes demonise those with whom we are in conflict, and that during the mediation process there are opportunities for seeing people once again as human beings, like ourselves, with similar feelings and needs. Transformative mediators call this process of seeing anew 'recognition', and mediators are encouraged to look for opportunities to encourage recognition between those in conflict.

Narrative mediation also encourages empowerment and recognition but puts more emphasis on the way we construct our stories about conflict. The process enables people in conflict to reframe their stories in the light of understanding and hearing other stories and interpretations.

Both styles, and indeed elements of other styles, find their way into the restorative process I shall describe, which relies on a very simple framework that can be adapted to suit the needs of the parties in the process. Essentially there are five stages:

Stage 1 – Establish guidelines and an agreed framework within which people can talk and listen to one another.

Stage 2 – Provide an opportunity for people to tell their story; to explain their thoughts at key moments in a conflict and articulate their feelings both at key moments in the past and at that moment.

Stage 3 – Identify what they need to move forward and explore the possibility of reaching a mutually acceptable agreement.

Stage 4 – If an agreement is reached, clarify what has been agreed, perhaps committing this to paper, and everyone present signing it as a gesture of commitment.

Stage 5 – Close the meeting with acknowledgement of the progress made, even if no resolution has been reached, and with an invitation to reflect on what to do differently in the future.

Preparation

Getting people to agree to mediation

Before going into more detail about the mediation format described above, it is important to emphasise that mediation is a voluntary process. People are unlikely to agree to take part unless they feel safe to do so and can trust the facilitators to create a safe framework in which they can get their needs met. Meeting with all parties before a mediation session is therefore very useful, although in a busy school day this can seem like an impossible ideal.

The other advantage of having a preparatory meeting with all parties (this is often the word used to describe those taking part in mediation) is that it can help people make some sense of their story, get in touch with their feelings and identify what they need to get out of the meeting. If this sounds very familiar, it is because the initial meetings are, in effect, restorative enquiries. In fact, since people may decide not to go ahead with a face-to-face meeting, the preparatory meeting may be beneficial in itself in helping people come to terms with a problem and find ways forward for themselves.

It is an issue of empowerment to acknowledge that if people choose not to proceed any further, and this needs to be an informed and considered choice, then this will undoubtedly be the best option for them at the time – regardless of what the mediator thinks. Mediators are unfortunately liable to believe so much in the virtues of face-to-face mediation that they can express disappointment if this is not the outcome, and believe they have failed. This is often the case in community mediation services and restorative justice units. Success is often measured in terms of the numbers of face-to-face meetings, and there is an uphill struggle to convince funders that an opportunity for restorative enquiry, leading to informed choice, is a positive, measurable outcome in itself. This is a relevant comment in schools too if projects are being funded by organisations requiring statistics for evaluation purposes.

The implications in a school when one person in a conflict has decided not to go ahead with a face-to-face meeting will depend on what else is available. It may be that fear prevents both sides from meeting and that the mediator can engage in a shuttle process, articulating perspectives, feelings and needs to and fro between parties. This requires skill and restraint, since misunderstanding of what one has been allowed to say, or a misinterpretation of the messages, can escalate the conflict.

In the event of a conflict that in the past would have been dealt with in a more punitive way, or where there is a risk of escalation if the matter is not dealt with in some way, then a school will need to have mechanisms in place for ensuring that all sides do get heard. They will need an opportunity to move on, even if it is not through any form of mediation, shuttle or otherwise. Restorative enquiry is again an option, perhaps used by someone in a more senior position to stress the potential gravity of the situation. The relationship between restorative interventions and more conventional behaviour management policies, with their tariffs of sanctions and rewards, is discussed in Chapter 8.

Setting the scene

If all sides have agreed to meet, and a suitable time has been found, then the next step is to set the scene. The room used needs to be one where there will be no interruptions and which is big enough to contain chairs of the same height. Regardless of the age or status of the participants or the mediators, having people sitting in different chairs creates unnecessary distraction and can convey unwanted messages of power imbalance. Mediation is an opportunity for people to meet as human beings, and put age and stage, status and power to one side in the attempt to find common ground, if possible.

The positioning of the chairs needs some thought. A triangle arrangement usually works well – people in conflict do not usually want to sit too close at first. If the mediator has arranged the chairs too close to start with, the chances are that, once they enter the room, angry parties will move the chairs a bit anyway. It is best to check at the outset.

Other practical issues to think about include:

- availability of water in plastic cups (glass can get broken and sharp edges are dangerous)
- availability of tissues in case anyone gets upset
- temperature and ventilation – if people are uncomfortable they may disengage
- proximity to toilets
- fire regulations.

Before starting the mediation proper people need to feel their needs are being met, and everyone must know that they can stop the process at any time to take a break, or indeed to stop altogether.

The mediation process

Stage 1: Establishing guidelines and agreeing a framework

Once people have arrived, and have been greeted respectfully and shown their seats, the mediator sets the scene by giving practical information as explained above, checks for comfort, and encourages agreement to stick to certain guidelines. Ideally parties in a conflict are invited to say what they need to get the most out of the mediation. Transformative mediators would argue that this is an important part of the empowerment process that gives back to people in conflict some control over their situation. I would not disagree. I would simply acknowledge that in my own experience people appreciate some ideas about the guidelines that have worked in the past. I have also noticed that very distressed or angry people, especially young ones, need some time before they take a very active part in the proceedings. Sitting listening to the gentle voice of a mediator explaining how things are going to work can help to calm people down and give them a sense of security. I tend to advocate that the mediators suggest the structure of the process. Participants are free to add or change things, provided this is acceptable to all sides.

In training, mediators explore what people in conflict are likely to need to be able to tell their story and get heard. This then informs the guidelines and also the explanation of the mediators' role. Usually the guidelines boil down to an agreement to let everyone have their say without interruption or challenge, to treat everyone with respect and avoid name calling or insults, and to try and keep what is said in the room. Sometimes a distinction is made between the agreement, which might need to be explained to others, and the personal details and feelings that might be shared. Ultimately these guidelines can only be suggested, but it can help to point out that the purpose of the meeting is to resolve the conflict if possible, and that too much talk afterwards could make things worse again.

Mediators need to explain that their role is to remain impartial and not make judgements; to refrain from making suggestions or coming up with solutions; to support the parties in finding their own ways forward; and to also respect confidentiality. The only proviso is that mediators need someone to debrief with and usually have a link teacher (if the mediators are students themselves) or a colleague with whom to talk about the case afterwards.

Stage 2: Hearing the stories

Essentially the mediator's role is to give each person an opportunity to:

- explain what has happened from their perspective, and what led up to it

- explain how they felt at the time and what they feel now

- perhaps talk about who else may have been affected.

This might involve the sorts of questions described in Chapters 3 and 4. The questions that were outlined in Tables 3.1 and 3.2 in Chapter 3 were used by the listener to help the speaker (a) sort out an issue for themselves, (b) get some understanding about what they had done or experienced, (c) consider the impact it had had, (d) reflect on what they needed to move on, and (e) explore what they could do differently another time. In Chapter 4 it was described as a set of questions that two people having a difficult conversation might use, taking it in turns to reply and judging when it was best to pose each one.

The mediation process is one in which the mediator might need to be making decisions about the order of questions at first, but that the goal is for the parties to take over the process for themselves by the end. After the mediation, especially in the small community of a school, people to need to talk and work together without a go-between.

The mediator may be making the initial choices because of the nature of conflict. People in conflict often blame each other and see each other as the problem. The role of the mediator is to help the parties recognise that the problem is a shared one and that they can work together to solve it. This is the stage when parties can begin to talk together and may not need the mediator at all.

The restorative enquiry process can help people in conflict to get in touch with their own situation and to get a better understanding of everyone else's situation. More often than not this can lead to all sides being prepared to work together on finding a mutually acceptable way forward.

What to ask whom, and when, are matters of judgement for the mediators. However, what follows is a structure based on the restorative enquiry process described in full in Chapter 3 (see Tables 3.1 and 3.2). The questions are repro-duced here, with some extra thoughts about what skills the mediator might need to use (see Table 5.1). I am calling this process 'restorative enquiry plus'. The extra skills (described more fully below) are:

1. Who goes first?

2. Teasing out the story.

3. Reframing.

4. Whether to dwell on the past or concentrate on the present.

5. Patience and empathy.

The mediator repeats this process with each person in turn. If more than two people are involved then it will be a judgement call about who to ask when. If everyone is sitting in a circle it might be appropriate to simply go round everyone in turn.

Table 5.1 Restorative enquiry plus	
Question	***Extra skill***
Can you explain what happened/what has been happening?	1, 2
(Mediator reflects back) So what I heard you say was…	3
What were you thinking at the time? How were you feeling at the time? How are you feeling now? (Mediator responds with empathy) Who else, apart from yourself, has been affected by the situation?	4, 5

1. Who goes first? It might be the person who first raised the concern about the conflict. It might be the person who indicates they want to speak first. It might be the person who seems least likely to sit still whilst others are speaking. The skill is in the judgement call. Pragmatism is necessary at times.

2. Teasing out the story. If a party is reticent, the mediator needs to think of some 'added value' questions that tease out the story without sounding like an interrogator or trying to meet their own agenda about what should be said. Examples might include:

- Can you tell me more?

- Would you like to say a bit more?

- Can you be a bit more specific?

- And then?

- And before that?

- And after that?

- Yes? (said with a rising, enquiring tone)

- … (silence – with an interested look on one's face!)

- repeating the last few words of the sentence can be useful.

3. Reframing. After each person has told their story the mediator will reflect back what they have heard. In Chapter 4 the skill of reflecting back like this was described as a useful conflict management skill. Here it can serve three functions: it indicates to the speaker that someone at least has listened; it gives them a chance to clarify if anything was unclear; and, if the story comes out in an angry and accusatory way, it enables the mediator to put it in a slightly less inflammatory way. This art is called 'reframing' and requires practice. The skill is to retain the essence of the statement, the meaning and the emotion, whilst enabling the other party to hear it. I like to use the metaphor of a picture with a frame so big and thick that the picture is obscured.

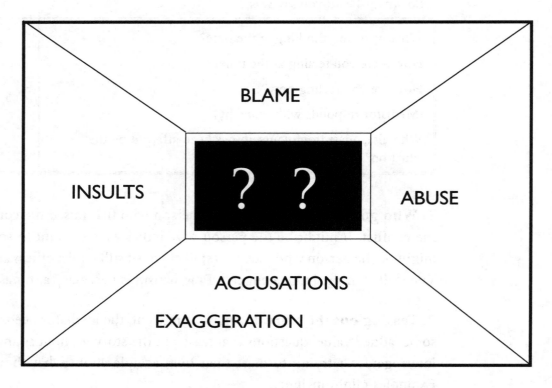

Figure 5.1 The metaphor of the picture frame – without reframing, the message is obscured

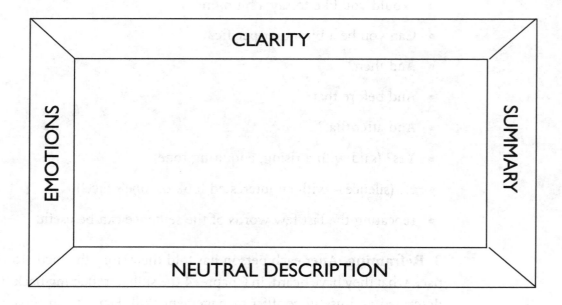

Figure 5.2 The metaphor of the picture frame – a clear message emerges

When the description of an event is full of blame, insults, abuse, accusations and exaggeration, the picture of what happened is unclear, and unlikely to be heard by the other party (see Figure 5.1).

The mediator may need to choose words that capture the strength of feeling and the essence of what has been said, and reframe them in a way that clarifies to both sides what is at stake. To pursue the artistic metaphor the new frame allows for the full picture to emerge and be seen by all sides (see Figure 5.2).

4. Whether to dwell on the past or concentrate on the present. The questions about feelings are, in many ways, more important than what has happened. The focus of restorative interventions is on who has been harmed by an incident and what they need to feel for the harm to have been repaired. This harm is described most vividly through the feelings of the people speaking, and what they need to move on grows out of these feelings. It is important to ask about the impact of the incident at the time, but in fact many conflicts between young people can concentrate on present feelings alone. This is a judgement call again and will, in part, depend how long the conflict has been going on and the perceived seriousness of it.

Once both sides have told their stories as fully as they need to, and have had a chance to express how they feel and acknowledge how the other person is feeling, it is time to move on to trying to repair the harm and move forward. A possible approach to this next stage, which I have called restorative problem solving, involves asking the parties to consider (using whatever phrasing is appropriate in the context) what they need (or need to do) so that:

- things can be put right

- the harm can be repaired

- they can move on.

5. Patience and empathy. Restorative problem solving relies on taking into account everyone's ongoing interpretations of what is being said (i.e. their thoughts in reaction to what they see and hear), the feelings generated by these interpretations, and their subsequent needs. The mediator may need to invite people to express these thoughts, feelings and needs at every stage in the ongoing discussion to ensure that an agreement is neither rushed nor imposed under pressure.

There can be no script for this. Patience, sensitivity, acute observation of participants' body language, impartiality and even-handedness are the key.

Stages 3, 4 and 5: Agreement, clarification and closure

Once everyone has expressed their needs, however unrealistic or unattainable, it is time to choose options that are practical and to which everyone can agree. The process of clarification can be a slow one, and the mediator needs to constantly check how everyone is. Minor disagreements over the details of an agreement can signal the fact there are still underlying tensions that may need to be addressed.

One problem-solving technique used by Jerry Tyrrell and the EMU (Education for Mutual Understanding) team in Northern Ireland is to use a flipchart and write up any ideas at all, however zany (Tyrrell 2002). The silliness of some of the suggestions can highlight more serious underlying needs. Wishing to see someone airlifted off the school playground by hot air balloon could indicate a fear of meeting them again in school, for example. Wishing to be on a desert island could also point to anxiety at being in school oneself.

'Being silly' can lighten the atmosphere, and sharing a laugh can be healing in itself. Once all ideas are gathered, people are invited to be a bit more practical, and often a sensible, achievable solution is found.

For the mediator, whose task is to record the agreement on paper if the parties request it, clarity is vital. People need to know what they have agreed to in terms of: Who does what? When? How? and What if it does not happen? There is a risk, if the agreement is written up later, that someone challenges what they have agreed to do. I have found it best to take more time in the session and ask if everyone will sign it before they leave. A photocopy is then given to everyone present, including the mediator. Finally, time needs to be spent checking what people have learnt from the experience and how they will behave if a similar situation occurs again, before the meeting ends with acknowledgement of the progress made and the hard work done.

'Victim/offender' mediation and bullying

There are times in school when the harm caused is undoubtedly the result of actions by a person or a group. Bullying is an obvious example in a school context. Situations involving someone who has been harmed and those who accept responsibility for causing the harm need to be treated slightly differently from what has been described so far.

Mediators need to be mindful that those who have been harmed by the incident could be affected in a number of different ways. Restorative enquiry is vital to ascertain how they are feeling and what they need, and assumptions about either could be damaging. Furthermore the needs of the people affected are paramount so that the process does not further victimise them. These people will need reassurance that meeting with those who have caused them so much hurt will be safe and likely to make matters better and not worse.

There is a potential tension between the value of a restorative meeting to those harmed and the value to those who have caused the harm. It is vital that a school using restorative processes is clear about the reasons for using them. Unless all sides are likely to benefit, then the processes can be harmful. It is worth stressing that restorative justice in school is not about using certain tools to tackle challenging and disruptive behaviour. If this were the case then those harmed by such events would be simply pawns in a process, put at risk potentially, for the 'higher good' of diverting wrongdoers from more mischief.

Why should a victim of bullying, or indeed of any harmful act, agree to meet the person who has hurt them, unless there is hope that they will walk away from the process feeling happier, safer and confident that the matter has been dealt with satisfactorily? Restorative processes must be voluntary on all sides. In fact there is growing evidence that such meetings can be beneficial all round. The Restoritive Justice Conferencing in Nottingham City Schools project, for example, has a lot of anecdotal evidence from students, their teachers and parents that they have all benefited from a restorative process. The bullying has stopped and young people have felt better about themselves.

My own experience in schools is that all sides experience huge relief to be given the opportunity to deal with an issue in a way that allows everyone to tell their story. It is a process that can appeal to the better nature of a young person who has, for a variety of reasons, fallen into behaviour that they themselves, deep down, may be feeling uncomfortable about.

It is often the case that people who engage in bullying activities are, or have been, the victims of bullying themselves. This is in no way to excuse or mitigate the impact of their actions on others. What it does highlight is that an impartial mediator, using empathy and treating everyone with respect, may be able to identify strategies that can prevent bullying recurring by meeting the needs of all the parties. We need to remember that the needs of those who have been harmed and the needs of those who have caused harm are very similar.

Re-victimisation

When someone has been harmed they need their situation to be taken seriously. Despite what was said about the mediator needing to keep an open mind, that does not mean suggesting to the person harmed that they may have some responsibility for what has happened. This would be highly inappropriate, and potentially devastating for the person concerned. Using bullying as an example again, it is still unfortunately the case that many young people have difficulty getting their situation taken seriously. The way in which a mediator deals with the case from start to finish can have an impact on the degree to which the harmed person engages and benefits. At no point would a mediator suggest that the victim of bullying was at fault, or in some way responsible for what had happened. This would add to the victim's distress and cause what is often called 're-victimisation'. Furthermore, when arranging a mediation session it would be important to establish whether those who had caused harm were prepared to acknowledge responsibility early on. Once again, using the mediation session to argue about responsibility could be very painful for the victim and make the situation very unsafe. It is a fine skill to protect the interests of a victim whilst remaining open to the possibility that there are issues beneath the surface that need to come out. (This has happened so often in my experience of mediation in schools that I believe it is important to stress it.)

I believe that the restorative enquiry process, used in preparation and as a basis for the mediation, is robust enough to deal with cases of clear-cut, admitted harm. The only differences might be in the time taken to tease out the story so that the full extent of the harm could sink in to those responsible, and the type of questions asked to explore repairing the harm. Those responsible for the harm would be asked: 'What do you need to do/what can you do, to repair the harm?' Those harmed would be asked what they needed for themselves, to move on, and so that things could be put right.

Is there a difference – does it matter?

The distinction between what I shall call here 'conflict mediation' and 'victim/offender' mediation is not as clear-cut in schools as it is in the wider community, although even there I have seen things get fuzzy at the edges. What distinguishes the two in the wider community is that the former tends to be used in neighbourhood and workplace conflicts that have not resulted in lawbreaking, whereas victim/offender mediation is offered when there has been an offence – an illegal act that has caused harm.

The fuzziness arises when what is against the law is described as an offence and what is legal is not, even though it can be harmful. For example, an offender of 17 physically assaulted a 12-year-old and damaged his jaw. He had undoubtedly committed an offence, and in the case I witnessed, the offender acknowledged he had a problem with anger. During the process it gradually emerged that the 12-year-old had said some very insulting things about the older boy's mother in his hearing. This did not excuse the violent attack. However, an apology from the younger boy, who acknowledged that his words had triggered the older boy's anger, meant that both sides felt their stories had been heard. Their need for justice and reparation had been met. It was down to the skill and sensitivity of the facilitator that an apparently 'open and shut' case involving a victim and an offender could have an outcome such as this.

I give this example because in school more often than not even 'victim/offender' type mediation might get fuzzy, as both sides begin to take responsibility for the impact of their actions on each other. A student sent out of class for swearing at the teacher might well, in an impartial atmosphere, acknowledge their 'offence'. However, they might well also want to explain why they behaved in the way they did, and this could mean explaining they were bored, did not understand or felt patronised. The words 'victim' and 'offender' are not appropriate in such circumstances. Here are two people who have fallen out, and both need to hear the other's side.

In case I seem to be labouring a point I will explain that there is increasing interest in introducing restorative justice into schools as a way of tackling disruptive behaviour and reducing exclusion. The emphasis is on using the process with students, and the implication is that, using the terminology of restorative conferencing, the 'disruptive' students are the 'offenders' and the teachers and other members of the community are the 'victims'. I trust that the way I am developing the themes in this book, with emphasis on whole school change, it is clear that I am not interested in restorative justice in schools simply as a tool to use on young people. As Marg Thorsborne said in her plenary address to delegates at the first International Restorative Justice Conference in Winchester in 2001: 'With restorative justice, *everyone* in school is accountable.'

That is also the message of this book.

The uses of mediation in schools

Bearing in mind what has been said above, what, then, are the potential uses of mediation in school? There are many uses:

- peer mediation for minor disputes between young people

- mediation by adults between young people in more serious conflict

- mediation between staff in dispute

- mediation between parents and teaching staff

- mediation between parents, LEA staff and their students (especially in cases of special needs, where a nationally supported initiative is being co-ordinated by Mediation UK)

- mediation skills training for parents to use at home.

It is useful for all members of the school community to have some awareness of the process of mediation, so they understand the principles and can appreciate when it can be used and its appropriateness. Since it is part of the restorative toolbox this information can be imparted as the project develops, using the school newsletter, assemblies, wall displays and perhaps an in-house video and other such methods of keeping people informed.

It is also important for all senior management, year and curriculum heads, teachers, classroom assistants and lunchtime supervisors to have training in mediation skills so they can use them on a day-to-day basis with young people, parents and colleagues. These are a natural development from the listening skills and one-to-one skills discussed in previous chapters. It is advisable that outside agency staff who deal with the young people on an individual or group basis are also familiar with the skills.

Finally it will be a matter of judgement how many young people receive the full training in mediation. Perhaps in time there will be a curriculum of conflict-management training, building on the Playground Peacemakers programme (Farrington 2000) at Key Stages 1–3, and leading to a recognised qualification in conflict management and mediation. For now, some schools choose to train a limited group of young people and others train a whole year group. In any case the regular circle time programme (discussed more fully in Chapter 7) will provide an excellent introduction to the key skills required, such as listening with empathy, recognising different perspectives, valuing diversity, developing emotional literacy and problem solving.

Young people can learn the skills of conflict management from an early age. There are schemes encouraging these skills at Key Stage 1 and 2 but mediation training is generally offered in primary and secondary schools rather than at infant level. (The early groundwork enables mediators to grasp the key issues more quickly so early work with infant-age children is encouraged too, perhaps using circle time.)

How much mediation is happening in school at present? In the next subsections I look at the extent in schools of:

- peer mediation

- mediation between teachers and young people and between colleagues

- mediation to repair acknowledged harm – 'victim/offender' mediation

- mediation involving parents.

Peer mediation

Peer mediation schemes are being developed all over the UK. There is a national network of young mediators of secondary school age, but not yet one for primary age mediators. Training is available from a variety of sources. Some local education authorities have behaviour support teams skilled and experienced in the training. Elsewhere, local mediation services offer schools-based training. Finally, there are private trainers whose names can be found in the directory of mediation trainers provided by Mediation UK. In my experience, young mediators dive into many situations adults may be more wary of, mediating between individuals in conflict, between groups and in situations where there has been harm caused and admitted. In other words, peer mediators often do not differentiate between what adults might describe as mediation, victim/offender mediation and group mediation/community conferencing. Their openness is an inspiration, but also flags up the need for the adult supporters to be equally flexible. At times these cases need to be referred on, and the adults will also need the flexibility to use whichever restorative process best fits the case.

Mediation between teachers and young people and between colleagues

The extent to which mediation is used in these contexts is unknown, and the information would be very useful. It would appear that teachers who have received training in restorative skills are more inclined to consider using the skills with colleagues and parents, rather than with students; but few records are available. I am unaware of systematic record keeping or data collecting in this field. However, it is early days. In the first chapter I referred to a paradigm shift in thinking that would be required to use restorative processes across a school community. The notion of general accountability, and the possibility of acknowledging mutual contribution when there have been difficulties involving adults and young people – these are both potentially threatening ideas. The challenge for restorative justice enthusiasts is to make the case for restorative dialogue to be just that – a process that restores good relationships, goodwill and well-being – and that must be a good thing for young and old in a school, or indeed in any community where people need to keep on working in proximity to each other day after day.

Mediation to repair acknowledged harm – 'victim/offender' mediation

The phrase 'victim/offender' mediation, and indeed the terms 'victim' and 'offender' are generally inappropriate in the school context. Nevertheless, as has been already discussed, the use of mediation in cases where harm has been caused by one person to another (perhaps significant harm as in the case of bullying) is of a different order from cases where there is interpersonal conflict and mutual recrimination.

Once again, records of such uses are hard to come by. The Restorative Justice project in Nottingham schools uses face-to-face mediation sometimes, but calls this process a 'mini restorative conference' because this is what the project is funded to run. In a project in a Berkshire school a restorative process is called a 'conference' regardless of the number involved. The terminology rather depends on the training received by the facilitator. Those from a mediation background call most face-to-face processes 'mediation' and those from a restorative justice background tend to use the term 'conference'. This makes the collection of information rather tricky. It is worth bearing in mind that there may be much more of a restorative nature happening around the country than we realise. It is just that people may be using different terms to describe it.

Mediation involving parents

There are various projects being developed around the country involving parents when they find themselves in conflict either with the school or with the local education authority, or both, over decisions made about their child. One example is the mediation being developed to help parents with children with special educational needs get the support they and the child need. It is now a legal requirement that all local authorities in England provide these services. Another example is the work of the African-Caribbean Home School Mediation Service in London that gives African-Caribbean families a voice.

There is undoubtedly a dearth of information about current developments round the country, and this is hampering further growth of restorative projects. Schools curious to explore new initiatives benefit from speaking to those in their area who have already started on the same road. Mutual support and encouragement is vital, and local support networks are a good way to generate energy and sustainability for new initiatives. The final chapter will explore the challenges of making a start in a relatively new field.

Training considerations

Training in mediation skills provides not only the tools to help others find creative ways forward in the event of conflict, but also enables people to:

- deal more effectively with relationships at home and at school

- enhance self-esteem and confidence

- develop assertiveness

- enhance listening skills

- improve articulacy and, by extension, literacy

- develop a set of tools for creative problem solving

- acknowledge that every behaviour is a choice

- take responsibility for the choices made.

The preparation for mediation is essentially a question of adding an understanding of the process described in this chapter with the skills of active listening and restorative enquiry. Training is usually done in the round so that participants get an experience of working in the circle. The circle also allows for a variety of techniques, from individual reflection, pair work, small group work, role-play and whole group flipchart work and discussion. Trainers vary in the extent to which they concentrate on the micro skills described – such as empathic responses, reframing, practising teasing out questions, and so on – as opposed to going in to role-play of the whole process almost at once and drawing out the issues from each role-play.

There is usually an emphasis on experiential learning – learning by experiencing something for oneself and having insights from this experience – rather than 'teacher-led' input. To my mind this is a truly restorative training approach, since it recognises that the answers to people's questions usually lie within the people themselves – and what is required is the supportive environment to discover the answers for themselves.

The following story, from an unknown source, was given to me by a teacher on one of my courses; it sums up the restorative training approach:

There was once a man who wanted to know more about jade. Through a friend he heard there was an expert on the subject living in the next village. The young man went to visit this person, an old man with a quiet, restrained manner. It was agreed that the older man would give ten lessons on the subject and a fee was agreed.

On the day of the first lesson the young man was shown into a room which was light and airy. He was invited to sit down and the older man gave him a piece of jade and left the room. The young man held the piece of jade in his hand, turning it around and wondering when the lesson would begin. After half an hour the older man returned and said that the lesson was over and showed him to the door.

The next week the young man returned for the second lesson and exactly the same thing happened. Indeed the same thing happened for several weeks and the young man was feeling increasingly frustrated and beginning to suspect he was being cheated.

Then one day he met the friend who had recommended the teacher. The friend asked how the lessons were going and the young man explained what had been happening week after week.

'And do you know,' he burst out angrily, 'last week he had the cheek to give me a fake piece of jade instead.'

Fortunately participants on mediation training courses do not usually go weeks before discovering their own inner wisdom on the subject of conflict. However, the principle holds good. The training is about creating opportunities for people to practise what they know, once given the opportunity to reflect on it. This might mean they replace what they thought they already knew with these new insights, but the knowledge has been grounded in the experiences provided by the training.

This experiential style works well with young and old. All ages also enjoy the harder work being interspersed with game-like activities that serve to raise the energy levels, change the atmosphere, and shift people around so they get a chance to work with someone new and have a laugh together.

I prefer to invite participants to develop their own scenarios – as in the role-play described in Chapter 4. This way I can be sure that what is being practised relates to the day-to-day experiences of those on the course. The only problem here can be that without experience participants do not always know the problems that can emerge. It can be useful to have a few spanners to throw in the works when people become more confident. There is an excellent little book produced by mediation trainers John and Diana Lampen called *What If's in Peer Mediation* (Lampen and Lampen 1997), which gives ideas for developing the 'what ifs' such as:

- what if someone is obviously not telling the truth?

- what if, as a mediator, I feel myself favouring one side?

- what if someone runs out?

Conversely role-play can often be far more challenging than real life and role-players have to be requested not to make things too tricky for beginners.

Training in the restorative skills described so far works best over a period of time so that participants have a chance to go back to school and try out their new-found skills. Each new week there is an opening circle where people can check in, and share their challenges and successes. It is wonderful hearing how excited people get when they discover that these processes really work. A participant recently, half laughing, complained about all the anger onions (see Figure 4.3) she found herself unpeeling with friends and family!

Case study – Mediation in the event of a conflict

Lucy and Emma, both in Year 9, fancied the same boy. Lucy challenged Emma about her behaviour and the two soon started arguing, both convinced that the boy was 'theirs' and that the other had lured him away. The situation would have got even worse, and indeed both girls later admitted that they were close to fighting, when one of their teachers stepped in and offered to mediate.

During the session both girls were able to explain how they felt, what had happened and what they actually wanted. In fact the situation was resolved; both understood that they had a lot in common. When I met them they were happy to talk about the whole situation, having become good friends as result of the mediation. Both girls valued the chance to talk to one another in front of a teacher who was neither taking sides nor reprimanding them for their behaviour. Both are keen to train as mediators themselves and help others in the way they had been helped.

Summary

This chapter has described a particular style of mediation that builds on the skills and processes described in earlier chapters. It has used the model of the interlocking circles of thoughts, feelings and needs, and behaviour as a basis for supporting people in conflict to find a mutually acceptable way forward, if possible.

It has differentiated between mediating between people in a conflict who may well each be seeing the other as the problem, and mediating when harm has been caused and acknowledged by one side. The chapter made the case for using an essentially similar restorative process, but with extra care taken to ensure that those harmed are not 're-victimised' by the process, or used as pawns in a process considered essentially as a behaviour management tool.

Finally, the chapter discussed the type of training best suited to developing the restorative skills of mediators. This builds on the examples given in previous chapters.

The focus of this chapter has been on a process that lends itself to smaller numbers. The next chapter pays greater attention to the requirements of a larger group process.

Chapter 6

Repairing Harm Through Restorative Conferencing

Restorative justice in schools provides empowerment for staff, teachers and students to have their needs voiced, their feelings heard, to heal harm if caused and to be included in the process of repairing damage.

Learning Unit Co-ordinator, Secondary School

This chapter considers the place of restorative conferencing in the whole school restorative approach. It describes what a conference is, what is involved in running one, and what it can achieve. It also considers the importance of thorough preparation and follow-up, and how to decide whether to use a conference or mediation in a particular situation. The process and the skills build on everything that has been described so far in Part II of this book and it will be clear that this is one more piece in the jigsaw of an approach underpinned by a common ethos and value base.

What is restorative conferencing?

Restorative conferencing is a process that seeks to repair the harm done to relationships within a community by an incident involving anti-social behaviour. It allows everyone involved to meet, and gain a better understanding from each other of the impact of the incident, the reasons for it and the preferred outcomes. The process usually involves the person or people who have been adversely affected, their parents/supporters, the person or people responsible for causing the harm and their supporters. Key school personnel and behaviour support staff may also be invited to attend, and indeed they may also have been personally affected. It has already been said in an earlier chapter that the terms 'victim' and 'offender' are rarely appropriate in school-based restorative conferences, and different schools use different terms. The objections to the terms include:

(a)   the labels are inappropriate when there has been no offence, in legal terms

(b)   labelling young people in this way can have long-term damaging effects, whether the label is 'victim' or 'offender' (the same objection can be made about a term such as 'bully')

and

(c)   restorative responses are focused on the actions of the person and not their very identity, and so labelling the person rather than the behaviour is incongruent with restorative values.

The conference takes place in a room where everyone can sit in a circle. Some thought is given to the seating plan and usually those people harmed sit with their family/supporters and those responsible sit with theirs. Other key personnel sit somewhere in the middle. Seating can be discussed in advance with all parties.

Ideally the facilitator will have communicated personally with everyone involved prior to the conference to prepare them for the process and to answer any queries and concerns. It is important that everyone present has volunteered to be there and that everyone feels safe. The conference is intended to be an ultimately positive experience from which people can walk away better able to move on and put the incident behind them. The purpose of the conference is to establish what harm was caused, what was the wider emotional context and impact, why the harm was done, what is needed to put things right and how the situation can be avoided in the future (Graef 2000).

The process is underpinned by the same model I have used throughout, with the focus on:

- What happened?

- Who has been affected and how?

- What can we all do to put things right?

The stages are the same as for the mediation process described in Chapter 5, but some of the focus would be a little different. My suggested model, figuratively outlined in Figure 6.1, is influenced by my background in both community mediation and the restorative conferencing model used by Thames Valley Police (2002).

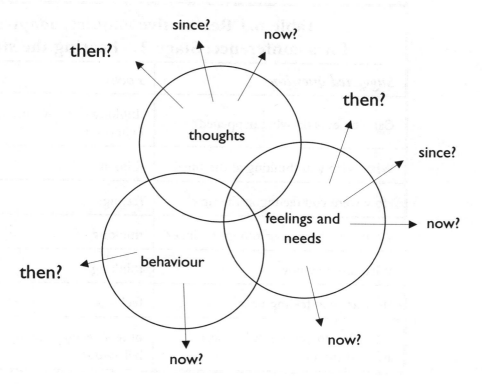

Figure 6.1 Restorative conferencing – the key questions

After guidelines are established and a framework agreed upon (Stage 1), in Stage 2 the questioning would be around the incident when harm was caused. The 'wrongdoer' will be invited to explain what happened and what they did, while the 'wronged' will talk about the harm that they and others have suffered. The word 'conflict' may be appropriate as well, but not necessarily. To suggest to the innocent victim of harmful behaviour that they are, or were, in a conflict with the person who harmed them could be upsetting and even accusatory. Nevertheless, and I say this cautiously, in the small community of a school, people interact with each other on a daily basis. Completely unprovoked harmful acts are possible, and do occur, but the non-judgemental approach of restorative mediation and conferencing creates opportunities to get beneath the surface behaviour to what may have provoked it. An important point to note here is that, unlike in mediation, supporters are invited to conferences and are asked how they have personally been affected.

Table 6.1 describes the type of questions that might be used in this stage of the restorative conference. Everyone develops their own style, and clearly it is disrespectful to ask a question if it has already been answered at another time, or if it is inappropriate at that moment. The model used in earlier chapters provides the inspiration for the type of questions and their purpose.

Table 6.1 Restorative enquiry, adapted for a conference: Stage 2 – hearing the stories	
Suggested question	*Focus*
Can you explain what happened?	thinking (interpretation) and behaviour
What were you thinking at the time?	thinking
How were you feeling at the time?	feelings
What have been your thoughts since?	thinking
What are they now?	thinking
How are you feeling now?	feelings
Who else do you think has been affected by this?	others' feelings, thoughts and behaviours

In Stage 3 the initial focus would be on what the aggrieved parties need so as to feel that this harm has been repaired, and then on what those who have caused the harm want to do to put things right (see Table 6.2). It is usual to ask the aggrieved parties to identify their needs first, to recognise their status as just that – 'the aggrieved'. It also helps those who have acknowledged harm to understand what they might be able to do to put things right. Sometimes young people who have done wrong seek to overcompensate because they are feeling so bad.

Table 6.2 Restorative enquiry, adapted for a conference: Stage 3 – moving forward	
Suggested question	*Focus*
What do you need (to do) so that: • things can be put right? • the harm can be repaired? • you can move on?	behaviour

Table 6.3 Restorative enquiry, adapted for a conference: Stage 4 – clarifying the agreement	
Suggested question	*Focus*
What do you think about X's suggestion?	thinking/feelings
What else would you need/to do?	needs
When/how/where will this happen?	behaviour
Would you like this written down?	needs

Stages 4 and 5 are difficult to predict and prepare for, as in the mediation process described in Chapter 5. The facilitator simply needs to be mindful, and keep checking on the thoughts, feelings and needs of everyone present as the discussion develops.

Table 6.4 Restorative enquiry, adapted for a conference: Stage 5 – recognition, rehabilitation and closure	
Suggested question	*Focus*
How can this situation be dealt with differently another time?	thinking
How are you feeling?	feelings
Is there anything else you would like to say to anyone here?	behaviour

In Stage 5 extra time may be needed for people to acknowledge the progress made and recognise that those who have caused the harm are beginning to take steps to make amends. It can be very hard to hear the impact of one's actions on others. People often express tremendous remorse and feel guilty and ashamed. A restorative process includes the possibility of restoring someone's self-esteem and self-worth, which is why, in some quarters, the conferencing process is described as one that encompasses 'reintegrative shaming' (Braithwaite 1989).

As I understand this concept, reintegrative shaming is different from the stigmatising and alienation that can happen when someone is simply punished and publicly condemned for their behaviour. This can either further alienate a young person completely or drive them into the school sub-culture of misfits, where there is a certain pride in non-conformity. A restorative process provides an opportunity for the wrongdoer to hear the full impact of what they have done on others – a painful experience which can generate feelings of remorse and shame – but then hear how those present in the circle acknowledge the steps they plan to take to make amends.

Those who have been harmed will also benefit, since they can witness the potential for change in those who have caused them harm. Lingering fears of reprisal, revenge or unpleasant gossip can make school feel unsafe. Genuine apologies and commitment to change can help everyone feel safer.

The skills used to run a conference are the same ones described in the chapters of restorative enquiry and mediation. The facilitator needs to be impartial, listening with empathy and ensuring all involved have an equal opportunity to tell their story, and have their feelings and experiences acknowledged. On occasion they may need to summarise and reframe what is being said. In a large meeting, with lots of people, this reframing will not always be necessary, or indeed desirable, since it does take time. A judgement call will be necessary.

The facilitator must be open to opportunities for giving increasing autonomy to the group. In an ideal conference those involved will do most of the talking by the end and the facilitator will remain quiet. However, the facilitator may need to interject if they observe that certain people are being ignored or becoming unhappy, angry or distressed by what is being said. The facilitator can steer the meeting back on course if necessary. What often happens is that the initial equal sharing of time and emphasis sets a precedent for the group, who themselves take responsibility for checking that everyone is in agreement as the discussion progresses. The circle starts to have a dynamic of its own.

An example of a restorative conference

This example shows the kind of judgements a conference facilitator might be making during a conference. I have taken an imaginary scenario, involving John, who has admitted bullying Mary. John has come to the conference with his mother and Mary has brought her father. Mary and John are in the same class and their form teacher is present, as is the year head (see Figure 6.2). Who to ask what and when is, to some degree, a matter of judgement. I will explain my reasoning in this situation at each stage.

The facilitator invites John to describe what has been going on first, to establish from the outset that he takes responsibility for what he has done. At this early stage he may not realise the full impact of his behaviour.

If his story is on the sparse side the facilitator may need to use some 'added value' questions along the lines described in Chapter 5. The challenge is to avoid sounding like an interrogator or asking questions with a judgemental

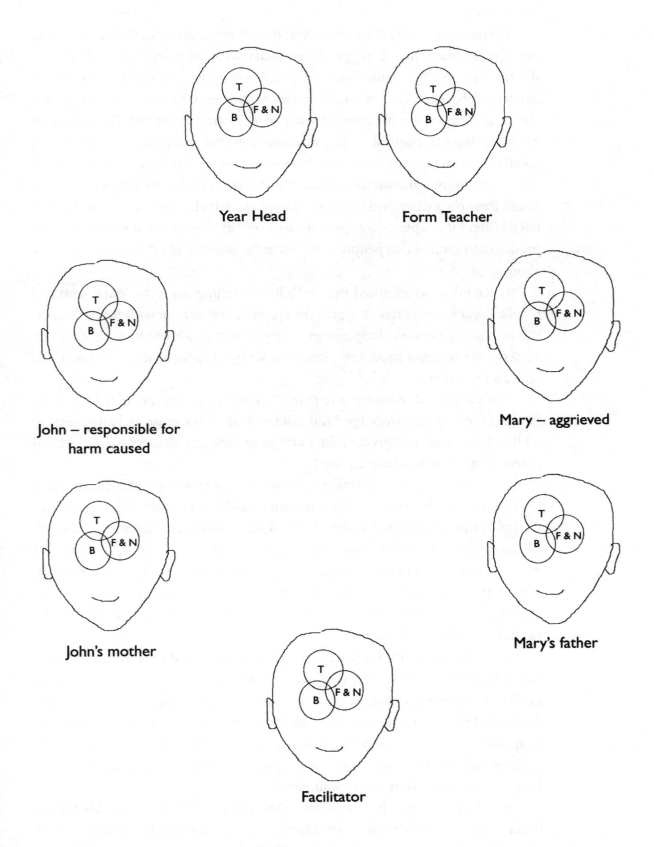

Figure 6.2 An example of a restorative conference in school

tone. (Some people might choose to start with Mary first to give her a voice at the outset.)

In situations where there are several people responsible for the harm caused, then the facilitator may draw out different details of the story from each of them in turn. Personally, I think this needs doing with care, especially if the people concerned have a different take on what happened, which is likely. There is a risk in getting drawn off course by apparent discrepancies and disagreements between those responsible. Such discrepancies and disagreements are almost inevitable if one subscribes to the theory that we all have our own individual interpretation of our own individual experiences. I prefer inviting each person to tell their own story, and note the differences, which may need to be clarified later. Different people do things motivated by different needs. It would be inappropriate to assume that people involved in the same incident feel the same way about it.

Once John has admitted responsibility by telling his story, Mary is invited to talk about her experience. Again the art is to draw her out without interrogating or making personal judgements. The guidelines, whilst merely guidelines, do serve as a restraint should facilitators be tempted to put in their own personal take on the event.

The purpose of this stage is to give Mary every opportunity to tell her story, have her feelings acknowledged and validated and make sense of it all to herself, whilst at the same time giving John perhaps his first opportunity to hear the full extent of how he has harmed her.

It seems appropriate in this conference to turn to Mary's father next. He is likely to be what in criminal justice parlance would be described as a 'secondary victim' in this incident and will probably want to express some strong emotions. Although guidelines for respectful language will have been agreed, it is, I believe, appropriate to allow people to vent their strong feelings along the way. The facilitator's role is to keep the conference on course, but not to stifle exchange and catharsis. If Mary's father chooses to address John directly, he needs to be allowed to do so.

Once the person (or people) harmed have spoken, and their supporters have had a chance to tell their story too, it is time to bring in other people. In this particular conference I chose to bring in John's mother early on. Others might decide to bring in the teacher and year head first. My choice, in an admittedly imaginary scenario, is that John's mother is likely to be holding in some strong feelings and, as a facilitator, I will notice this and make a judgement about how long she can hold these in without blowing!

It can be hard for the supporter of the person who is responsible for the harm to hear the full details of what has happened, and how those harmed have been affected. They may also have some difficult emotions to grapple with. Supporters react in different ways. Some will want to defend their young person, others will join in the condemnation at this stage or express their own distress, disbelief or disappointment. Alliances can form between parents across the circle and these can be useful as agreements are explored later. Of course inter-family feuds and rivalries can also come to light. Much of this will have been discovered at the preparation stage, which will be discussed later in the chapter.

Once John's mother has spoken it is time to hear from the school representatives. In preparation the facilitator will have invited the teacher to speak from a personal perspective if possible. This may seem risky to the teacher, since it is often the case that teachers are used to hiding behind their professional mask, for understandable reasons. Nevertheless, the teacher is almost inevitably going to have views and strong feelings about the incident. Their authentic response, coupled with their genuine concern for both young people, is likely to be a key component in the outcome of the process. Involving teachers as human beings with feelings and needs, rather than as professionals with views and judgements, is one of the unique features of a restorative process, at any level. The involvement of the year head is a matter of judgement. Once again this person can be invited to express their personal feelings about the incident. However, they may also be invited to represent others in the school and the school's official view of what has happened.

In the early days of using restorative conferencing it is likely that existing behaviour management policies are still in place, as are policies regarding bullying. What is, or is not, an excludable offence may still be playing a part in the choice of outcome. In Chapter 8 the relationship between restorative approaches and traditional behaviour management policies is discussed in more detail.

This incident, and the presence of the year head, highlights the possibility that the outcome of the conference at an inter-personal level may need to be weighed against the official school line. The year head is going to be wearing two hats.

Incidentally, in such a conference, a member of the senior management team may choose to be present instead of the year head. In the early days of a project this would be wise, until school policies across the school have been brought into line with restorative philosophy, and the whole senior management team, and the governors, are on board. It would be disastrous for all concerned if the agreement reached in a conference was ruled out of order or unacceptable by someone more senior in the school.

Once everyone in the circle has had the opportunity to speak, the facilitator returns to John. He is asked if has understood the full impact of his behaviour on everyone present and anyone else who has been mentioned. He is given an opportunity to say what he would like to do to repair the harm and then the whole conference moves on to this healing stage.

Mary is asked what she needs in the first instance. It may be that, in his reaction to what he has heard, John spontaneously apologises to Mary and others. If Mary has heard this apology, and judges it to be sincere, she is unlikely to ask for it again. If she has not heard it or believed it, or needs to hear it again, then some sensitive handling of the issue is called for. Apology under pressure – 'Would you like to say sorry now, John?' – could do more harm than good. Restraint is needed as everyone explores what they need.

Even if everyone in the room thinks John should apologise, and John is not ready to, or able to, at that moment, then he should not be forced to do so. However, in the climate of rehabilitation and reparation other positive things may happen and the facilitator needs to be patient, without expectations of their own.

Clarifying the agreement can take time, and, as discussed in the chapter on mediation, the facilitator may need to keep checking on the thoughts, feelings and needs of all those in the circle. On the other hand, by this time, the circle may have its own internal dynamic and the facilitator is simply keeping a watchful eye on proceedings.

Their contribution may be needed if a written agreement is required and the task then is to ensure that everyone is clear on exactly when, where, how and by whom actions are to be taken and that what is written is agreed and signed by everyone. (A photocopier nearby would be handy at this stage so everyone can take away a copy.)

Once the agreement has been clarified, recorded and signed by all if required, time needs to be taken for everyone to acknowledge what has happened in the meeting, and how they feel. It will not have been an easy experience for anyone. Difficult things will have been expressed and heard. Those responsible for harm, in this case John, may well be feeling extremely bad about themselves. If they have begun to make amends and committed themselves to some form of reparation, this needs to be acknowledged. If no one else does this then the facilitator might. However, at the risk of manipulating the situation, if an opportunity is given at the end, it may be possible that others in the circle will say something helpful.

Restorative processes are not soft options, but they are meant to contain within them opportunities for healing and moving forward. If those responsible for the harm caused leave the meeting feeling very bad about themselves, without any support, encouragement or recognition from others present, then:

- they may well experience exactly the same sense of alienation as someone who has been punished in other ways – or perhaps even more so

- word is likely to get around that the process is definitely to be avoided by other wrongdoers

- there is still a potential for further harm, due to the unresolved bad feelings.

After a final check round the circle to see how everyone is, remaining open to the possibility that there may still be some unresolved issues, the facilitator will thank everyone for their time and close the meeting. If refreshments can be made available this gives an informal opportunity for everyone present to resume a more 'normal' relationship with each other.

Running a restorative conference

Preparation for a conference

Perhaps it can be seen from this detailed analysis of a particular conference how important the preparation for a conference is likely to be. In the ideal world the facilitator will make time to talk to everyone who is to attend to prepare them for what is to happen. Using restorative enquiry, people are helped to order their thoughts and also get a flavour of what is to happen. People are unlikely to agree to attend unless they know what is to happen and how it is to happen. The facilitator needs to be using all their restorative skills at this stage, including impartiality, empathy and active listening, and thus demonstrate what people are likely to be experiencing in terms of process.

Preparative restorative enquiry *is not* about:

- sympathising with those who have been harmed

- expressing disapproval to, or about, those who have caused the harm

- telling people what will happen in terms of outcome, or even hinting at it, for fear of making false promises

- persuading or pressurising people to attend

- telling each party what others have said unless expressly asked to do so or given permission to do so.

Preparative restorative enquiry *is* about:

- in the first instance, simply letting people talk about the incident and how they are, without reference to any further steps

- empathising with the feelings expressed by everyone

- remaining impartial, whatever one feels personally about the incident

- explaining the potential of a restorative meeting and how it works

- exploring any reservations people have about taking part

- accepting whatever choice is made, with respect

- if a meeting is agreed to, ascertaining what guidelines need to be in place for discussion to happen, and gaining everyone's agreement to these in advance, based on an understanding of the purpose of the meeting.

Conducted in this fashion the preparatory restorative enquiry can be beneficial in itself, just as in the case of mediation. It may be all that is needed by some people.

Follow-up

Any restorative process is merely a snapshot in the lives of all those involved. The true impact of a restorative intervention will only become apparent over time. Those who have caused harm will need time to demonstrate that they mean what they have said. They will need the trust and support not only of their immediate community – their friends and family – but also of the school community.

In the event of reparation agreements certain people at the school are likely to be responsible for ensuring the agreement is honoured, with contingency plans if it is not (which may well be a further restorative meeting to ascertain what has gone wrong).

During the conference certain issues may have come to light that need further attention – such as extra academic support, problems at home, issues to do with anger or drug-taking. The facilitator will need to be working within a clear set of guidelines so that everyone understands what will happen. Since confidentiality is an important consideration, conference participants will need consulting if issues are to be followed up. If the preparation has highlighted certain issues it might be pertinent to ensure that a relevant person attends the conference to offer support and information.

Schools will need to have clear protocols for the follow-up issues to ensure that facilitators do not bear the responsibility for this important part of the whole process. In any case, facilitators will need to have someone they can debrief with after a restorative meeting, to help them review their own practice and raise any concerns.

Who is the appropriate facilitator?

Every school is likely to come to a different arrangement on this issue. It has already been explained in the chapter on mediation that students themselves can be mediators. A primary school in Nottingham uses young people to run conferences too. In a secondary school in Berkshire some year heads are trained as conference facilitators, and they run the conferences involving issues between the students and on occasion between students and teachers. In Devon, Police Youth Affairs Officers run conferences in the secondary school to which they are attached. In a new project in Banbury teachers and learning support assistants from one secondary school and its feeder primary schools are exploring the possibility of working as a team, and calling on each other to run conferences in each other's schools to help with impartiality.

There is no tried and tested formula in this new and developing field.

Mediation or conferencing?

I have said in an earlier chapter that the process used in schools partly depends on the resources available and the background and training of those developing the restorative project. When I first began mediating in schools I was a firm believer in helping the young people sort matters out for themselves. I would therefore advocate face-to-face mediation for most problems, simply involving the key players. This has the virtue of being relatively quick to set up and does not involve complications over availability.

However, I now believe more and more in the value of involving parents and teachers where possible. There are several reasons for this:

- If parents or teachers are not involved, they may object subsequently to the outcome of a mediation.

- With parental involvement there is more chance that young people will take the matter seriously and realise that their actions impact on their family too.

- If the issue is one that spills out of the gates into the community, there is a chance of resolving bigger issues that would not be resolved otherwise.

- Some people would argue that without the involvement of the wider community the process is unlikely to be fully restorative. Certainly parents and teachers can play a supportive role subsequently, as can other students in the school.

- The process is educative, and the involvement of parents and teachers helps to spread the message wider, and perhaps suggests alternative ways of dealing with issues in the classroom and at home.

Of course, when the incident is one involving young people and adults anyway then all sides will need appropriate support. In the example of John and Mary it may have also been necessary to invite a younger supporter for each student so the meeting is not overwhelming. This would need to be explored with the participants.

If one has the luxury of having facilitators confident with all forms of restorative intervention, from restorative enquiry to running a large conference, then the choice of process comes down to appropriateness and pragmatism. The appropriateness will in part depend on the wishes of those involved and on the nature of the incident. The pragmatism relates to who is available, how soon the process needs to be run, how long the process is likely to take and how much time is available.

What sort of issues could be dealt with using a conference?

In the project in Nottingham already referred to on several occasions, the following incidents are highlighted as ones that can benefit from a conference:

- classroom disputes falling short of outright bullying

- bullying incidents where the school wishes to use restorative justice

- disruptive behaviour by one student

- minor damage to school property where there has been no official complaint

- minor theft when there has been no official complaint

- minor public order incidents where there has been no official complaint

- common assault where there has been no official complaint

- name-calling/teasing/taunting

- harassment

- non-attendance.

It must be stressed that in this project, as far as I know, the process is being used to deal only with issues defined as those where young people are responsible for the harm caused. I have already emphasised that there is potential in the process for discovering that there may be responsibility on all sides. In an increasing number of schools, conferences are being used instead of fixed-term and sometimes permenant exclusions. When exclusion has occurred they are also being used on re-admission.

Training issues

A competent restorative practitioner, with the flexibility to run whatever restorative intervention or process is required by the circumstances, will need to combine the skills of an active listener, a restorative enquirer, a mediator and a conference facilitator. In training, the skills described and developed in Chapters 3–6 are introduced sequentially and practised in increasingly demanding role-play situations. By the end of a restorative skills training programme a participant should feel able to offer facilitation in any situation that involves people meeting to share experiences, address a problem, resolve a conflict or repair harm.

One thing that training should teach is that the less facilitators and mediators say the better. If they limit themselves to only what has been suggested here, or indeed at times even less, the process is likely to be of some benefit. If they begin to offer advice, express opinions, deliver mini-lectures or ask questions to find out things they themselves want to know, then the process may well disintegrate. These are all practices I have used as a teacher myself, in the mistaken belief that it was what was needed at the time.

Case study – Restorative conferencing

Becky and Mandy were at the centre of a long-running conflict that was beginning to affect the whole year group. Sides were being taken and the year head was at her wits' end as to how to resolve the situation. She mentioned the situation to the police school liaison officer because she had heard about restorative justice and thought a conference might be the answer. He contacted the local Restorative Justice Unit, who rang me.

Usually I prefer to approach everyone concerned myself from the outset, but in fact the year head made all the arrangements. She had a very good understanding of the role of the mediator in not taking sides or pre-judging issues. I think her conversations with both girls and their mothers were sensitive, and contributed to their willingness to meet to try and sort the matter out.

I suggested that I had a private word with each girl and each parent before the actual meeting, to help them organise their thoughts, get a sense of what everyone wanted from the meeting and establish some rapport before we started. During these meetings I noted how the two mothers experienced the situation in similar ways. Both were struggling to care for the family on their own, fed up with the constant quarrels, and eager to get to the bottom of the matter. In many respects the two girls also had similar stories. Both regarded the other as the one to blame, but both were also keen for it all to stop.

Once I had listened to all four and also briefed the year head on her role (essentially to speak as herself and to explain how the situation was affecting her and others in the school), we gathered in a small office which was just big enough for us to sit in a circle.

During the meeting the similarities I had noted in the preparation came to the fore. Both mothers established a connection because they recognised a shared frustration over their daughters' arguments. Although both had previously accepted her own daughter's version of events, it became clear to both mothers that each girl was responsible for keeping the conflict alive. Having the mothers present helped the girls to realise just how much they had affected not only themselves but their whole family. From the year head they learnt that many others were being drawn in and that in fact there was potential for everyone to put the matter behind them. Both were also able to talk about how they had been affected and about the issues behind the initial quarrels. Worries about being included in friendship groups were shared, and both girls explored how to help each other, and also how to explain to their friends that things had now changed. The year head offered support and an opportunity to review the situation in the future.

Both mothers and daughters left the meeting visibly relieved, and the year head was delighted.

Case study – Conference to address a bullying incident

Leanne, a year 7 girl, had been on the receiving end of some bullying behaviour since starting at her new secondary school. Present at the conference were Leanne and her mother; Sharon, who had been causing Leanne's distress (also in year 7); Sharon's father; the police officer to whom the matter had been reported; and myself. The conference went well. It became clear to the 'victim' and her mother that their own loving, supportive, relatively affluent family was what both the 'bully' and her father did not have. The father was struggling to make ends meet and raise the family and, feeling let down by life, took things out on his daughter for whom he did not have a single kind word. When Sharon found herself in a supportive, non-judgemental environment, and felt that her own story had been heard, she was able to appreciate the distress her behaviour had caused Leanne and her family. She made a genuine apology and plans for future friendship and support were made. The police officer offered Sharon's father information on local support available for single parents. In the final closing 'go-round' I asked if anyone had anything else they wanted to say and the jubilant original 'victim', clearly visibly relieved and elated, said: 'Whooppee!' I think that just about sums it up.

Summary

This chapter has focused on restorative conferencing, describing in detail a format for running one, the type of questions asked and the judgements that a facilitator makes in deciding whom to ask what and when to ask it. Although suggested phrases are given, the process is quite flexible and everyone will adapt it to suit their own style and, more importantly, to suit the needs of the situation. It may be objected that even the guidelines described in this chapter are too prescriptive. But in training hundreds of prospective mediators and conference facilitators I have become convinced that people need an initial structure to keep them on track.

The chapter has highlighted the importance of thorough preparation for a conference and sensitive follow-up after such a process. It has also considered who might be an appropriate facilitator and how to identify when to use mediation and when to use a conference.

Restorative enquiry, mediation and conferencing invite everyone in a school community to consider new approaches to old problems. Focused training in restorative skills can be useful. However, there are many types of circles that can be used in the school on a regular basis which also provide opportunities for skills development and practice. The following chapter looks at how these circles fit into the overall scheme of a restorative school project.

Chapter 7

Circles

Restorative justice provides an opportunity for empowerment – *your* voice can be heard.

Primary Learning Support Assistant

Sitting in a circle with members of one's community, most of whom share a common interest in restoring harmony, care, safety and respect to that community, is the starting point for many restorative practices. Advocates of restorative justice draw inspiration from Native American peacemaking circles and the community problem-solving traditions of Maori peoples in New Zealand (Johnston 2002). However large or small the circle, the principles remain the same.

This chapter considers the place of circles in a whole school approach to restorative justice. It begins by suggesting that regular circles, across the school community, form the seedbed from which can grow the restorative skills and approaches described in the book so far. Restorative justice works best when there is a commitment to community, where there is already mutual respect, a willingness to listen to each other, a need to belong and be included. This cannot be taken for granted in any modern community and cannot be taken for granted in a school. In order to have a community, and relationships that people want to restore, we need to work to create that community in the first place, and the relatively discrete community of the school is an ideal environment to start.

The chapter advocates regular circles for every part of the school community and describes the different roles the circle can play. It considers the community building potential of circles as well as its uses when there are problems to solve in groups or even large group conflict.

Circle time

Working in circles in the UK is often given the name 'circle time' and has many enthusiastic advocates (e.g. Bliss *et al.* 1995; Kingston Friends Workshop Group; Mosley and Tew 1999). These people have produced excellent books full of ideas and activities to support the busy teacher wanting to develop a circle time approach. It is not my intention to duplicate some already excellent resources. My intention in this chapter is draw out the links between circle work and restorative practice. I would argue that the skills and ethos of restorative practice can be developed in a school through circles and that without regular circles it will be difficult to maintain the ethos vital to successful restorative work. Although the writers mentioned above suggest circle time for staff and students alike, most of the ideas in their books tends to be for use with young people. I cannot emphasise strongly enough that a whole school restorative approach relies on every member of the school community having the opportunity to meet regularly in a circle with their peers and to develop together the skills and ethos required to develop a strong, supportive school and team spirit. From this 'restorative seedbed', processes such as mediation, restorative debriefing, conferencing, restorative discipline procedures and win-win problem solving develop naturally. Without such a seedbed the processes mentioned above are merely tools – with no well-nourished roots and no sustainability.

Circle time is a popular process used in primary schools and, increasingly, in secondary schools. It provides an opportunity for people to come together in a safe, supportive and enjoyable way to learn more about each other, to grow together as a team, to develop communication skills, to share exploration of problems and to celebrate achievements. Participants are able to develop their social, moral and emotional skills and develop a sense of shared purpose. In process and content circle time embodies the spirit of inclusion and develops active citizenship skills.

Using games, pair and group activities, circle time can help to develop self-esteem, appreciation of others, listening skills, problem solving, co-operation and a sense of fun. It is not just an educational and enjoyable experience for young people, however. All members of a school community can use this process to enhance their working relationships – whole staff teams, senior management, lunchtime controllers, governors, to name but a few.

In my experience however, not enough time is spent on developing the safety and trust in a circle before embarking on some of the wider applications of circles, such as conflict management, team building, personal and social education and emotional literacy development. I have seen young people attempt some potentially risky discussions without firm guidelines in place and without the safety needed for a certain amount of disclosure. Circle time is not a therapy session. However, well run, it can provide a forum for sharing worries and problems in a relatively safe way. For such a forum to work, the facilitator needs to know what they are doing and have clear guidelines and boundaries in place.

I would maintain that circle time needs to be underpinned by the same principles and values that underpin all restorative approaches. The guidelines in the following boxes are essentially the ones I offer to those embarking on circle time for the first time.

Circle time – Guiding principles for running a good session

- Circle time is, above all, fun. Never forget the games! Laughing and playing together builds trust and a sense of belonging.

- Circle time is developmental – the skills required to make the most of the circle are learned by taking part.

- Sitting in a circle, on chairs of the same height, in an airy room where there will be no interruptions or people doing other things, is, for me, essential. Everyone can then feel included and the focus of attention is into the circle.

- The facilitator encourages everyone to take responsibility for the smooth running of the session by asking them to identify some simple guidelines that they will need to take part. This would be a session in itself if your group has not already done this.

- The facilitator is not responsible for the 'discipline' of the group once the rules have been negotiated: everyone in the group is. If someone is unable to respect the rules I would stop the session, explain I was feeling uneasy and ask how everyone else is feeling (as a 'go-round') and then ask for ways forward. I would encourage respect for the feelings of those who appear 'disruptive' and endeavour to offer alternatives to the circle if it is proving challenging for them. (Reprimands and sanctions are not congruent with the spirit of circle time, to my mind.)

- Everyone has the right to 'pass' on a go-round or a game. No one must feel under pressure to contribute, but in time most people feel safe to do so. This may take weeks though. Sitting in the room but not in the circle would not be an option as far as I am concerned, however. Do you have a colleague who could welcome someone who really does not want to join in at all?

- The facilitator says as little as possible. Making a comment after each contribution by a participant is an abuse of power! Encourage participants to deliver their comments to the circle, not to you. A talking stick highlights how often any one person talks – it certainly shuts *me* up!

Restorative value base for running circle time

- A commitment to mutual respect, which means that all 'put-downs' are discouraged, and challenged if made. (It is vital that the facilitator keeps positive and respectful at all times to model this, however frustrated they may feel!)

- An acknowledgement that we have the right to feel what we feel. There are no 'shoulds' and 'shouldn'ts' about feelings. A feeling is a feeling – but we might need to think about how we express the feeling in order to be heard.

- An acceptance of the right of others to a different point of view even if we disagree with it.

- An openness to working with people we may not usually work with, so we can develop tolerance of diversity, even in our own classroom or staff room.

- A commitment to respecting our differences and celebrating our shared experiences.

- An awareness of the shared responsibility for the good running of the session.

- An acceptance of the shared responsibility for including everyone and a sensitivity to each other's feelings about feeling excluded.

- An understanding by everyone that not being able to respect circle time rules is not being 'naughty' , 'disruptive' or 'unhelpful', but evidence that a need is not being met and something else is required to enable that need to be met.

- A belief that the content and process of circle time need to be congruent so that what we are saying and what we are doing fit!

To emphasise just how valuable this process is for adults I would invite readers to imagine what a team or department meeting would be like if it were run as described above. My suspicion is that we have all had experiences of meetings being dominated by people who talk too much, imposing their views on others without due regard for their views and feelings, and with the real views of the quiet ones only being expressed afterwards, between clenched teeth, in small groups in the cloakroom or the pub.

Readers may balk at beginning team meetings with games, and of course these are not always necessary. However, a sense of fun and a relaxed, safe atmosphere is often important, and I have run many circle time training sessions in which the feedback suggested that the games helped the staff to achieve this – a rare opportunity. Of course the rationale in such circumstances was always that staff needed to play the games themselves to be able to play them with their students, but I know from experience that adults will benefit personally as well.

Circle time acknowledges the importance of feelings, yet this side of ourselves is all too often deemed unprofessional in meetings. Nevertheless, if we are unable to express what we are feeling it leaks out in other ways. Restorative communication emphasises the need to be able to express what we are feeling and what we need in a way that is heard, without it being destructive or harmful. In the early stages of using circles for meetings this may not always be easy, but providing time is taken to acquire the skills, the meetings can only get better. This is what is meant by the principle of learning through taking part.

The values and principles underpin the circle experience and need to be understood and modelled by the facilitator in the first instance. However, the management of the circle process needs to belong to the participants, which is why negotiating guidelines at an early stage is vital.

In Chapter 2 I described how to negotiate guidelines in an introductory meeting about restorative principles. I use the same process with adults and children alike at the beginning of a circle time programme.

As mentioned in Chapter 2, the guidelines, or rules, grow from people's need for well-being and safety. Not only is everyone consulted and their views heard, but seeing the rules in terms of well-being helps people to see that breaking a rule will, by definition, impact on somebody's well-being. In other words, our actions have an impact on others. If we have a need, and some would argue a right, to feel safe, then we have a responsibility to maintain that right for others too.

Negotiating guidelines at the beginning of a year

Young people, and indeed people in general, engage more readily with rules or guidelines that they have developed themselves and for which they can see a point. Once the guidelines have been agreed it is easier to see that breaking a rule does have a significant impact on the well-being of others in the group. This is a first stage in encouraging young people to see that each action is behaviour with an impact and that we have choices about how we act. I hope it goes without saying that the guidelines established by the group apply equally to the adults working with the group. Adult teams may wish to develop their own guidelines and the same procedure described in Chapter 2 works well with them too.

The point to make is that these are the things we need, as a group, to work at our best. If we are not getting them, then we are not working at our best. The responsibility of the group is to ensure that everyone is giving each other what they need.

Working with the groundrules in circle time

The groundrules need constant review – they are the mission statement of the group for working harmoniously together. Preventing conflict is preferable to picking up the pieces afterwards – although every conflict is an opportunity for learning conflict management, so it is not desirable to avoid conflict all together! In Chapter 2 I suggested a simple sentence completion activity; this can be used repeatedly, over several weeks, concentrating on a different guideline each week to help the group realise what they all need from each other. Examples of sentences to pass round:

> *I don't feel respected when…*
> *I do feel respected when…*
>
> *I don't feel safe when…*
> *I do feel safe when…*
>
> *I don't feel valued when…*
> *I do feel valued when…*

I have picked these examples because the need to feel respected, to feel safe and to feel valued are some of the more common needs on a list.

The facilitator generally starts the activity. In this way they are taking the first risk, not asking people to do anything they are not willing to do themselves and modelling the nature of the contribution. Another circle time convention is that no one has to contribute, and so the right to pass is introduced early on. If a talking stick is being used for this activity then it can simply be held for a short spell and passed on, or the word 'pass' can be said. It is always a good idea to go round a second time because often people who passed on the first round have had time to think and can now contribute. There is no pressure, however. Sometimes a 'pass' can mean someone has nothing to say or is not in the mood to take part at that moment. The emphasis is on feeling safe at all times, since it is only when we feel safe that we can take risks.

Doing this sentence completion activity regularly highlights the different needs we have, even though we seem to be asking for the same thing. 'Support' from one person can feel like 'interference' by another, for example. It also helps young people develop a practical repertoire of things they can do to meet the needs of others. The guideline 'valuing each other' becomes more meaningful when we know that a teacher, for example, loves to be thanked for an interesting lesson or a shy student is thrilled to be greeted by her name. It can lead to some very practical changes in behaviour that no one has really given much thought to before.

One staff group was struck by the idea that they all need to feel valued and respected and yet had a staff room in which everyone had their own personally labelled jars of tea and coffee. Somebody suggested that they adopted a system of shared refreshments and that on the wall, by the kettle, should be a list of everyone's tea and coffee needs. In this way, when one person saw another in need of a 'cuppa' they knew exactly what drink to make and whether milk and sugar were required. This suggestion made a significant impact on the feeling of staff solidarity and care.

Rule making through game playing

When working with younger groups and people with short concentration spans I suggest playing games straight away, and introducing the idea of guidelines through the games. Explain a game and then ask if any rules are needed for the game to work (e.g. if it involves swapping chairs, what rules might there need to be to make it safe?). Once a few rules have been suggested, ask if everyone agrees. After the game, review whether people were able to stick to the rules or if any more were needed. Maybe try the game again. Variations on the game could also be suggested and tried out. Important questions include:

- How can we ensure people do not feel left out?

- Is the game safe or might someone get hurt?

- How can we mix up boys and girls?

- Is this game possible for all abilities in the room? Do we need to make adjustments so it can be? (For example, swapping seats is difficult for someone in a wheelchair.)

Listening to everyone's contribution is vital, so early on you may need to ask students what they need from each other to be able to take part in discussions. Whenever you ask for contributions it may be worth considering asking students to work in pairs before inviting contributions in the open circle. Speaking out is daunting, and sharing some ideas with a partner beforehand builds confidence. It also ensures that everyone gets their ideas heard by someone, even if they do not get a chance to talk in the wider circle.

Respecting the guidelines

At some point someone will raise the question about what happens if the guidelines are forgotten or ignored by someone. If the school is deciding to embrace a restorative approach in dealing with rule transgression then the response is straightforward. What is at stake is that by failing to adhere to one of the rules, others have been adversely affected. Clearly the way forward is for those affected to meet and hear from each other how the situation has impacted on them and for all sides to agree an acceptable way forward. This approach takes time so here are some quick suggestions for dealing with problems as they occur.

1. Respond at once by expressing how the situation has affected you and what you need to move on and then by asking the other people involved what happened from their perspective and what they want to happen. This can often lead to a quick resolution with no residual bad feeling.

2. In the middle of a circle time lesson this approach can be widened out to the whole class to great effect because it demonstrates how thoughtless behaviour in a room is likely to have an effect on most people in the room.

Try using a 'go-round' starting with yourself:

> *When someone talks loudly during the lesson I feel angry because...'*

Then invite all the circle to complete the same sentence. Be prepared for some not to feel the same way as you!

Now go round again and maybe start with what you would like to happen in general terms but without making practical suggestions at this stage. See what comes from them, and in particular those whose behaviour has been causing you distress. You are appealing to their better nature – this is a 'no-blame approach' in action:

> *What I would like to happen is...*

I have found this approach can help all the class to take the responsibility for the smooth running of the lesson and have not needed to use it very often.

3. Failing this, arrange for a longer conversation with those involved after a lesson when tempers have cooled and people have had time to reflect. Be prepared to hear the reasons behind the behaviour and what the students needed that they were not getting at the time. Explore with them how these needs could be met in a different way and encourage reflection on how to deal with a similar situation next time in a way that does not cause you or them distress.

Remember the emphasis all the time is on:

- What is the meaning behind the behaviour?

- Who has been affected by the behaviour?

- What was everyone feeling and thinking then and now?

- How can the harm caused be repaired?

- How can the matter be put right as far as possible to everyone's satisfaction and so that people's needs can be met?

- What can be done to avoid the same situation happening again?

4. Sometimes conflicts flare up between others when you are not directly involved. In such situations mediation might be required. Circle time is the foundation of effective mediation, sharing the value base of mutual respect, listening to all sides, being non-judgemental and respecting that those in a difficult situation are often the best ones to resolve it.

The key point is that if the guidelines are for everyone, then ways need to be found for dealing with rule breaking that are acceptable and useful for everyone involved. Naming, blaming, shaming and punishing need not come into such an approach and might not be welcome by the adults in any case! (And never were welcomed by young people.)

A circle time structure

A great deal of time has been spent discussing the negotiation and reviewing of guidelines for the group, because in essence the circle time experience is *about* being in a group and community building.

Every activity, even the most playful, is an experience of being with others and interacting in a positive way. Every experience shared in the group is an opportunity for learning more about human interaction. If someone feels left out, or that their opinion is being ignored, then review of the activity in which this happens allows for people to hear how that experience feels, and whether they have contributed to it.

However, the circle time programme needs careful thought if it is to be an enjoyable experience for everyone and not become too much like navel-gazing. My guiding principles come from the iceberg/mountain model considered in Chapter 2, with its underpinning values of high self-esteem, affirmation of others, communication and co-operation. At the end of a circle time session everyone will, ideally:

- feel better about themselves

- feel better about each other

- have had an opportunity to express themselves

- have had an opportunity to listen to one another

- have worked or played together co-operatively

- have reflected on what they have learnt and enjoyed.

The programme needs to create opportunities for as much of this to happen as possible. I would argue that in a restorative school, striving for the mountain rather than the iceberg, these aims would be written into every lesson.

A circle time session might comprise:

- **A gathering** – a go-round in the circle when everyone makes a very small contribution, maybe completing a sentence suggested by the facilitator.

- **A mixer** – a game that ensures everyone mixes up and sits with people they do not usually work with.

- A slightly longer **focus activity** on a particular theme (listening skills? negotiation skills? planning? private reflection and drawing? citizenship issues?).

- **A review** of what has been learned as a circle go-round or in pairs.

- **Another game** if time – preferably a co-operative one.

- **A closing** – 'One thing I have enjoyed this time...'

The type of circle described above can be fitted in to most busy weeks, either as part of the literacy hour, since it undoubtedly supports language work, or as part of the citizenship and PHSE (pastoral, health and social education) programme or in the tutorial slot most secondary schools allow for. The time is valuable for creating a sense of belonging in a class group and encouraging them to develop an ethos of care and responsibility towards one another.

It lays the ground for developing the restorative skills described earlier in the book, and most training in such skills is run using the circle format.

Problem-solving circles

There are times when a particular issue or a problem facing a group needs to be discussed. If a group is used to circle conventions and feels safe to talk in this way, then circle process is ideal at such a time. The facilitator 'holds' the circle, ensuring everyone has a chance to have their say, perhaps passing round a talking stick.

If emotions start to run high then the facilitator will use such skills from restorative enquiry, mediation and conferencing as they feel are relevant.

Problem-solving circles might be used by:

- governors

- teaching staff

- parent groups

- learning support teams

- lunchtime teams
- school councils
- class groups
- sports teams.

The list is endless. The only point to make is that such groups are unlikely to be very successful if the members of the circle only meet when there is a crisis. There are schools in Berkshire that regularly start the day with a staff circle, so that everyone can check in on each other, share problems and ask for support if required. One school invited me in to run a circle for staff just before an OFSTED inspection. Fears were shared, help was asked for and offered, and people spoke later of how helpful it had been. Perhaps all teachers need regular circles to get themselves through an inspection.

Again in Berkshire there are plans to extend the existing circle time programme, which focuses on the children, to include adults' circles for parents and others for learning support assistants. The aim is to develop the confidence and assertiveness of such groups so they can have a real voice in the school.

Community conferences

To some extent, a community conference is similar to a problem-solving circle. Once again the words are not necessarily important. What is important is the ability of the facilitator to be flexible, and use the skills required by the situation. In the school context a community conference might be used when there are conflicts developing between large groups of young people or there is disharmony in a class group, a staff team or amongst parents.

The facilitator would be using circle conventions, while mindful of the conference structure and the need for everyone to express their thoughts, feelings and needs once they have told their own story. In large groups it would be usual for facilitators to work in teams of at least two.

There are no rigid guidelines for such processes. Small group discussion might need to precede the large group meeting; break-out meetings might need to be held during the meeting. Preparation beforehand will of course be vital, as will a clear set of guidelines at the outset. Nevertheless the skills of restorative enquiry and the strength of the circle will provide the keys to a successful outcome.

Family group conferences

The use of family group conferences as part of the restorative jigsaw in a school is being pioneered in Hampshire. They are a different type of problem-solving circle but rely on the key restorative values of empowerment, inclusion and the belief that those with the problems are best placed to resolve these problems. They can be used whenever the behaviour of a young person is causing concern and it is felt that the wider family network could be useful in supporting the young person. More often than not, in such circumstances, the immediate family group is in need of wider support. The co-ordinator of the conference (in Hampshire these are from the local education authority) spends time communicating with the immediate family, the young person themselves and whoever this person identifies as potential sources of support. Family members and friends of the family are helped, financially and practically, with travel to the venue for the conference, which is usually a neutral venue chosen by the family as suitable for their needs. Professionals with concerns about the young person are also invited to the meeting.

Initially the coordinator chairs the meeting and time is allowed for the professionals to raise their concerns about the young person and for the family to ask questions. After this the co-ordinator and the professionals leave the room and the family are left to agree a plan for the young person's care and protection, and also decide how this plan will be reviewed and what to do if any part of the plan is not carried out.

When the plan has been agreed the co-ordinator and the professionals return, the plan is recorded and resources are negotiated. A plan would only be rejected if it was felt that the young person was being put at risk (see Morris and Tunnard 1996).

There are many different situations in which this variation on the restorative conference process can be used in the school context. Examples include in the event of non-attendance or when a young person's behaviour looks likely to lead to exclusion.

Case study – A problem-solving circle

An early experience of discovering the power of circles took place when I was the tutor of a Year 7 group at an inner-city comprehensive many years ago now. The school was on the edge of the city, in an area that was predominantly white. Most of the students came from council estates and were friendly, street-wise and good-natured in their tolerance of the teaching staff who were, after all, doing their best!

At the beginning of the school year I put aside the tutorial programme I had been given to follow for the first few weeks of the term. Instead, I concentrated on giving the young people the task of working out for themselves how we might organise the sessions in such a way that everyone could have their say and feel listened to. We negotiated groundrules but also, importantly, the class discussed the best seating plan for such activities. It took several tutor periods for them all to agree, and they chose a circle format. Not as I would have liked – normally it would have involved moving the desks aside every time; however, seating places were aranged around the outside of the room, leaving desks as they were, so that some people sat on desks, some on chairs and, from a bird's-eye view, a circle shape was approximated and everyone felt included.

The whole process took many weeks, and a lot of trust had been developed over this time. They had learnt to respect each other's views and appreciated that I was sharing power and responsibility with them. The space must have felt safe enough for Leroy to decide to share his problems with the group. A boy of about 12, Leroy was a likeable, extrovert lad who certainly made his presence felt in every class. His energy level and mischievous nature did not find favour with everyone and he was beginning to get into quite a lot of trouble. What his class-mates and I had not appreciated was that he was also coming in for some targeting from other students because of his colour, and possibly for his challenging behaviour.

I cannot remember if he was the only black child in the school, but he was certainly in a tiny minority. My suspicion is that he had developed a rather larger-than-life persona to cope with this situation, which was also the same at his junior school. Be that as it may, he poured out his troubles to his classmates who listened respectfully. And then they took it in turns to explain to Leroy how they experienced his behaviour towards them.

Leroy heard how they did not always appreciate the way he spoke to them, or the way he handled situations at times. Gradually, during this extraordinary tutor group session, the whole class negotiated how they would support and stand by Leroy in the playground and in lessons if he, in turn, tempered his own behaviour towards them. Everyone acknowl-edged that no one deserved to be the butt of racism, and all of them were more than happy to help Leroy challenge this, but they were also clear that his troubles were not always necessarily caused by racist attitudes.

The issues that were raised were complex – but these were Year 7 students speaking from the heart, and what they resolved together was brave and honest. Leroy left the room walking six foot high, and this was very important. He had felt heard, and so had everyone else. I was moved, and very, very humbled.

Summary

This chapter has described the various uses of circles in the school context. It has made a case for circles being at the centre of a whole school restorative approach and the conventions of the circle becoming the way a school does business.

It has described how the increasingly popular technique of 'circle time' fits into the restorative jigsaw and differentiates between this more formalised process and circles held to address problems and concerns. Both have their place in the timetable of students and staff alike.

Meeting in a circle is the starting point for every restorative process, whether it is a circle of three or 20. Meeting in circles regularly can provide an opportunity for every member of the school community to:

- recognise their role in that community

- take responsibility for the impact of their actions on everyone else in the community

- be supported by that community

- work together in resolving any problems people have in the community

- celebrate belonging to that community.

This chapter has explored different applications of circles, ways of establishing safety through groundrules and ways of addressing conflicts when they occur in the circle.

In the next two chapters, which look at issues of implementation and sustainability, circles remain at the heart of the process.

Part III

Implementation and Sustainability

The last two chapters consider the issues of implementation and sustainability of a restorative project in a school. In some respects both chapters touch on both issues, but in different ways. Chapter 8 considers the policy that needs to be in place to sustain the restorative approach – a relationship management policy rather than one that focuses merely on behaviour. However, one could argue that it will be impossible to begin to implement a restorative approach throughout the school unless and until there has been a review of existing strategies and policies for dealing with conflict and inappropriate behaviour.

Chapter 9 reflects on recent evaluation of restorative projects and highlights recommendations for both implementation and sustainability. The main focus of the chapter is on a five-stage model that enables schools to begin the implementation process in such a way that sustainability is written into the development plan from the outset by virtue of making in-house capacity building a key feature of the plan.

Chapter 8

The Just School – A Punishment-free Zone?

> Restorative justice provides all involved with the opportunity to heal harm done to others.
>
> Secondary Learning Support Assistant

Preceding chapters have described an approach to conflict and inappropriate behaviour that is at odds with the way many schools currently deal with such matters. This chapter begins by differentiating between a school that focuses on managing behaviour and one that focuses on maintaining relationships. It makes the case for a relationship management policy rather than a behaviour management policy (see Cameron and Thorsborne 2001). It goes on to pull the various strands together to support a school in developing a coherent and consistent framework for addressing challenging issues as they occur and reducing the likelihood of them occurring in the first place. It makes a case for developing the policy on relationships as a whole school community. It refers to examples from the rest of the book of how to do this and emphasises the point that the whole approach needs to be informed by the values and ethos of restorative justice. In keeping with restorative philosophy, the chapter is not prescriptive. It does, however, offer suggestions on how to proceed and what might need to be considered for a policy to be congruent and enabling, educational and developmental for every member of the community, young and old.

Managing behaviour – Barking up the wrong tree?

Schools in the UK are required to have a behaviour management policy. These policies focus, by definition, on behaviour. The emphasis is on encouraging good behaviour with incentives and discouraging unacceptable behaviour with sanctions. This emphasis is based on what William Glasser would call 'external control psychology' (Glasser 1998). This approach is widely used in homes, schools and the workplace by those in authority with those over whom they have power, or for whom they have a responsibility. It is an approach that can often be effective in ensuring people behave in ways the authority figures believe to be appropriate. However, whilst it might be desirable for people to behave towards each other in a pro-social way, being coerced to do so means they are doing the right thing for the wrong reasons. To behave well in order to be rewarded – whether this is with a good grade, a merit mark, a prize or a certificate – encourages self-centred motives, and dependency on others' approval. It does not help to develop an internal locus of control and an ability to take responsibility for the behavioural choices made and the impact these choices have on others. When the reward ceases to have value, the individual can cease to perform in the way that the reward was intended to encourage (Kohn 1999).

To behave well in order to escape punishment also encourages selfishness, since 'the focus is on oneself rather than on others' (Morrison 2002). The consequence of inappropriate behaviour is often described as something unpleasant happening to the miscreant. In fact, the true consequence of inappropriate behaviour is that other people are harmed and that the relationship we have with these people is harmed. Furthermore the underlying message of punishment and the threat of punishment is highly questionable – 'If you hit your sister again then you will feel the back of my hand.' How often do adults punish children with the very same action that the child was doing in the first place? Even in the more civilised sanctions in school, be they exclusion from the classroom, a detention or a visit to the headteacher's office for a telling off, the message is similar: 'If you do what I, the more powerful person, do not like, then I will do something unpleasant to you.' It is no surprise that we see young people everywhere doing or saying similarly threatening things to each other.

What follows is a series of questions that can be useful to consider with a staff team who are attached to their existing behaviour management policy, with its system of rewards and sanctions, despite the fact that it is meeting neither their own needs nor the needs of the young people. The questions can be put to small groups of people, each group supplied with several large sheets of paper and plenty of coloured board markers.

The activity described has been developed from ideas shared with me by two restorative practitioners in Australia who remain great sources of inspiration, Peta Blood and Marg Thorsborne. The whole activity generates a lot of discussion, since it is often the first time that whole staff teams have had the opportunity to share their thoughts with each other on these issues. So often teachers are isolated in their classrooms and have no idea what their colleagues are doing, or what they think about what they are doing, beyond the level of the staff room gripe.

For the purposes of this chapter I am going to take each question in turn and discuss the typical responses to each one. In practice I would give each group plenty of time to write their responses to one question before moving on to a fresh sheet and a fresh question. At the end of the whole activity I would encourage the groups to lay the sheets side by side and consider the relationship between all of them and what conclusions they come to. A recent variation I have used is to give every individual a sheet of paper and invite them to fold it into four columns. The first question is then written at the top of the left hand column.

Question 1: What are the sorts of (serious) behaviour you currently have to address in this school?

It can be useful to start with what is considered in the school as the more serious incidents, although the activity is relevant even for minor misdemeanours. Typical answers can include:

- fighting
- persistent disobedience
- repeated disruption of lessons
- bullying
- verbal abuse of teacher
- physical assault on teacher or student
- carrying weapons
- smoking cigarettes
- drug use
- repeated failure to do homework.

Question 2: What are the meanings behind these behaviours?

It is important to acknowledge at the outset that there is no necessary connection between a behaviour and its underlying meaning. People react in different ways for different reasons. However, what is at stake here is an attempt to put words into the mouths of young people if only they were able to articulate their needs. Often misbehaviour is, to use Marshall Rosenberg's phrase in a wider context, 'a tragic expression of an unmet need' (Rosenberg 1999). It is useful to phrase the meanings in terms of the phrase 'I need' whilst acknowledging that the people exhibiting the behaviour may not be able to articulate the need in this way. Examples from recent workshops I have run include:

- I need attention.
- I need friends.
- I need to hurt someone, because I am hurting.
- I need someone to listen.

- I need power.

- I need to feel in control.

- I need a hug.

- I need love.

- I need help with my work.

- I need challenging.

- I need something interesting to do.

- I need to belong.

Question 3: What are my current responses, or the responses of the school, to these behaviours?

It takes courage to admit to some of the answers to this question, because we often react in ways we know are not necessarily the most appropriate. To my shame, I am the first to admit that I have shouted at young people, lost my temper, sent them out of the classroom and dispensed detentions as if they were sweets, in my chequered career as a teacher. I knew then, and I know even better now, that these were extremely ineffective ways of dealing with the situation. I was immediately aware of the negative impact this was having on my relationship with the young person in particular and with the rest of the class in general. To my credit, I was also frequently available for young people to talk to me, we developed groundrules as a class and we shared strategies for dealing with things together. In other words, I sometimes did OK, and got it right, and sometimes I didn't! These admissions can help people to feel safe to share their strategies and, once again using examples from recent workshops, the answers can include:

- shouting

- threats

- bribery

- making time to listen

- sending out of room

- moving to a different chair

- detention

- exclusion – fixed term or permanent

- keeping in during breaks

- referral to department or year head or senior manager

- letter to parents

- distraction

- a quiet word in the ear.

Question 4: What are the ideal outcomes I am hoping for with this response?

Answers from recent workshops include:

- making sure others can learn/play

- restoring harmony to classroom

- regaining control of the class

- asserting my authority

- teaching person a lesson

- diverting person from behaviour

- teaching them a different way

- getting to the root of the problem

- getting on with my lesson

- setting boundaries

- setting an example to the others.

It is interesting to look at the answers to Question 2 and Question 3 and consider which of these responses address the needs that might be behind the behaviours listed in Question 1. If I am running the activity, I invite groups to look at the connections between the two relevant sheets. If the activity is being done by individuals, I invite them to draw links themselves and then compare with a partner. Some connections are shown in Figure 8.1 using the examples I have given. It is usually the case that only a few responses actually do meet the underlying needs and the more punitive ones rarely do.

It is also interesting to consider whether the current responses do in fact achieve the ideal outcomes hoped for. Figure 8.2 shows some possible connections. None of the ideal outcomes are expressed in terms of restoring relationships and reconnecting the young person with whoever may have been affected by their behaviour. The one outcome on the list remotely restorative – the desire to restore harmony – is admirable, but excluding someone from the classroom does not achieve harmony. That can only happen when the relationship between the student and the teacher, and between the other students in the room, is repaired. What can be even more illuminating is looking for a response that both

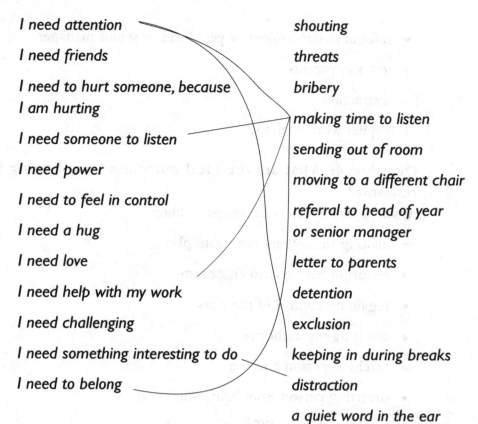

Figure 8.1 *Connections between the needs underlying inappropriate behaviours and responses to those behaviours*

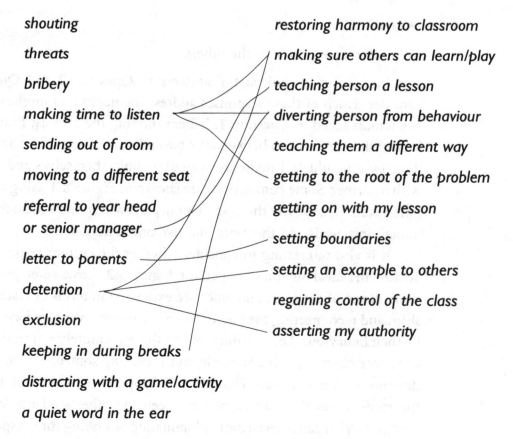

Figure 8.2 *Connections between responses to inappropriate behaviours and ideal outcomes*

meets the needs behind the behaviour and achieves the outcomes sought by the adult responding to that behaviour or by the school as a community.

One example from the answers given in Figures 8.1 and 8.2 is that the need for attention, the need to belong and the need for a listening ear is met by someone taking the time to listen, and such a response might achieve the objective of getting to the root of the problem and diverting someone from their current behaviour.

At this juncture it can be useful to ask a fifth question:

Question 5: What are the underlying beliefs and assumptions behind our current responses to misbehaviour?

This can be an extremely uncomfortable question to consider. Answers may include:

- When someone does something wrong they deserve to be punished.

- Punishment or fear of punishment changes behaviour.

- Teachers need to be in control of their classroom.

- Punishment teaches compliance.

- An example needs to be set.

- Boundaries need to be set and maintained by sanctions.

It would appear from these common responses that the general belief held in schools by most teachers is that a discipline system needs sanctions and that this is how justice is done. This view mirrors closely the belief of society at large in respect of offending behaviour and what constitutes justice. If we consider our society's response to serious offenders and a school's response to very disruptive students, we see a similar response: 'Our criminal justice system locks them in. Our school system locks them out' (Thorsborne 2003). In neither case are their needs met, unless the offenders or the students find themselves in a restorative environment once they have been locked in (to a young offenders' institution) or locked out (and referred to some form of alternative provision). In neither case are the needs of the people they have directly affected by their behaviour addressed. In neither case is the wider impact of their behaviour on friends, family and the rest of their community dealt with. In neither case is the harm caused to their relationships with all of these people healed or even considered important. By focusing on behaviour, a key principle of restorative justice is ignored – namely that crime, or misbehaviour, is essentially a violation of people and relationships (Zehr and Mika 1998). Furthermore we know from recent Home Office research that there is a high correlation between excluded children and street crime. Schools may lock disruptive young people out. It might not be long afterwards that the criminal justice system then locks them in. It is to be hoped that restorative approaches developed in both schools and the youth justice system will ensure far fewer young people are either locked out of school or inside young offenders' institutions.

People need to belong

A key theme through this book is that relationships need to be at the heart of all school policy. We know, from asking people what they need from each other to work at their best, that an important issue is the need to belong, to feel part of a team, to be supported and to feel valued as a person (see Chapter 2). Recent research on adolescent health in the United States indicates that feeling connected can greatly reduce the risk factors that lead to anti-social and self-destructive behaviour (McNeely, Nonnemaker and Blum 2002):

> When adolescents feel cared for by people at their school and feel like part of their school, they are less likely to use substance, engage in violence, or initiate sexual activity at an early age. Students who feel connected to school in this way also report higher levels of emotional well-being. (p.138)

To ensure connectedness in a school everyone needs to be mindful of opportunities for building, nurturing and, where necessary, repairing relationships. Relationships are central to good working practice, effective classroom management, successful teaching and learning and safe, supportive, inclusive school communities. Part of this connectedness is taking responsibility for the impact of our actions on each other and caring about this impact. Compliance with pro-social guidelines in a community needs to come about through understanding and a sense of community and not be seen as an end in itself (Thorsborne 2003).

A paradigm shift?

In Chapter 1 I referred to the work of Howard Zehr and mentioned that in his early writings on restorative justice in the criminal justice field he alluded to the possibility that what was at stake was a paradigm shift in thinking about how to deal with wrongdoing. I suggested that one was perhaps also necessary in schools. So many schools use a system of rewards and sanctions for managing behaviour in young people that it has become almost inconceivable to think that there may be another way. Figure 8.3 shows a questionnaire adapted from Howard Zehr's original paradigm for a school context. The left-hand column focuses on rules and behaviour, the right-hand column focuses on repairing the harm done to relationships.

Many teachers who have seen this paradigm say that they do not think the two columns are mutually exclusive, and that different responses are required in different situations. It remains to be seen whether the two approaches are indeed compatible. Current debate in the criminal justice field has advocates for

Retributive or restorative: What are your current views?

The central column represents a 1 to 5 scale. Please indicate your opinion by circling 1 (strongly agree with retributive attitude), 2 (mildly agree with retributive attitude), 3 (unsure), 4 (mildly agree with restorative attitude) or 5 (strongly agree with restorative attitude).

Retributive	1 2 3 4 5	*Restorative*
I would define misbehaviour as an action that involved breaking the school rules or letting the school down.	★ ★ ★ ★ ★	I would define misbehaviour as harm done to the well-being of one person or a group by another or others.
In dealing with an incident I would want to find out what happened, who did what and who is at fault.	★ ★ ★ ★ ★	In dealing with an incident I would want to find out how all sides are feeling and what they need to put things right.
When a young person has misbehaved it is my responsibility to decide what to do, or to refer it to a senior colleague who will decide.	★ ★ ★ ★ ★	When a young person has misbehaved I believe in dialogue and negotiation so that everyone involved has an opportunity to communicate and co-operate with each other.
When a young person has misbehaved s/he needs to be punished so as to deter him/her from doing the same thing again.	★ ★ ★ ★ ★	When a young person has misbehaved s/he needs to acknowledge his/her contribution in what has happened, make amends and identify how to avoid something similar happening in the future.
The behaviour management policy of the school/unit sets out the appropriate responses to misbehaviour and need to be applied consistently.	★ ★ ★ ★ ★	Misbehaviour is often a symptom of, or a reaction to, interpersonal conflict from which all sides can learn to do things differently. Therefore every situation needs considering separately.
Sanctions need to be in place for misbehaviour.	★ ★ ★ ★ ★	All those involved in an incident need to decide how to repair the harm done, if possible, and sanctions are inappropriate in this context.
The person who misbehaves is the focus of my attention. I do not involve those affected by the misbehaviour in deciding the way forward. This would not necessarily be appropriate.	★ ★ ★ ★ ★	I encourage all those affected by an incident to consider the way forward, if at all possible. This might include students, parents, teachers, classroom assistants, and other staff.
Someone who does wrong deserves to be punished. Once that has happened the matter is closed.	★ ★ ★ ★ ★	Someone who does wrong needs to acknowledge what s/he has done, understand the impact of this on others, be involved in finding a way to put things right and explore ways of doing things differently next time. The matter is closed when all those involved think it has been dealt with fairly and satisfactorily.

Figure 8.3 The paradigm shift questionnaire: Assessing attitudes about how to deal with wrongdoing

replacement of the current retributive system with a fully restorative one. Others say that we need both and that restorative justice needs to be integrated into the current system. Schools will need to decide for themselves if any situations merit retribution. It would appear that once people have been convinced by the arguments of restorative justice, and, importantly, once they feel confident to use restorative skills with even the most challenging of behaviours and the most complex of situations, they find it difficult to contemplate a return to retributive approaches.

It needs to be said that the restorative approach to inappropriate behaviour is not the soft option that some people believe. Becoming accountable to one's fellow students or to colleagues, friends and family for the impact of one's behaviour, and to be required to make amends, can be an uncomfortable experience. The difference between a punitive response and a restorative response is that the former can stigmatise, isolate and alienate someone who may already feel disconnected, whilst the latter has the ultimate goal of re-integrating the wrongdoer back into the school community.

Inventing a unique set of wheels

Every school is different, and requires a different approach. It is relatively common practice, in my experience, for schools to borrow each other's policies as a basis for developing their own on the grounds that there is no point in re-inventing the wheel. This chapter argues that inventing a new and unique set of wheels together, as a whole school community, is a vital part of developing a restoratively inspired relationship management policy. In fact it might not be too easy to find a school with such a policy in these early pioneering days. However, even in a few years' time when, with luck, all schools are convinced that this is the way forward, it would not be advisable to borrow each other's policy.

In Chapter 1 I referred to a whole school approach as a jigsaw of interlocking parts but also as a wheel in which every spoke had to fit and be in good repair. Designing, building and maintaining this wheel, or set of wheels, is the role of the whole community if the school is to keep on moving forward. The principle of involving all those whom it concerns in developing their own set of guidelines for building, maintaining and repairing relationships is congruent with restorative values. Pragmatically as well, every school is unique and requires a unique approach. So many factors combine to make it so. Social, political, economic, religious and geographic factors can influence what is expected from a school from outside the school gates. The make-up of the school community is different, with adults and young people each bringing their own personalities, ethnic backgrounds, cultural and social expectations, learning and teaching styles, emotional and physical needs and life stories into school. Furthermore, every school has its geographical and social idiosyncrasies, depending on its location in the country and in its immediate community.

Finally, every school has its unique design features and layout, and these impact on the way people in the community use the buildings, move about within them and relate to each other. A coherent policy on how people live and work together in this special place will grow out of all these factors being taken into consideration, and the only people who can really understand all this are the people who are there – the members of that school community.

Starting from the value base

In Chapter 1 I emphasised the importance of ensuring that the restorative values inform every aspect of the school day, and that they underpin all restorative skills and processes. In Chapter 2 I described a process to use with groups to explore what values they share in common and to link these with the restorative project. The following list of values, mentioned in these chapters and referred to again frequently throughout the book, is a long one. However, the list serves as a reference point when elaborating policies. Whatever policies and practices are used in the school they need to relate to this list, or else it is likely that more harm than good will result in the long term. (See Appendix D for a photocopiable version.)

- Mutual respect
- Trust
- Openness
- Empowerment
- Connectedness
- Tolerance
- Integrity
- Congruence
- People have the need and ability to resolve their own problems
- Acceptance of diverse experience and points of view
- Valuing one another
- Acknowledgement
- Encouragement
- Listening
- Sharing ideas
- Acceptance that mistakes happen and we learn from them
- Importance of feelings, needs and rights.

Whether a school reviews its current policy or decides to start afresh, the checklist can help to keep people on track. Whatever strategies or approaches are agreed they need to be underpinned by the value base.

Are people's needs being met?

In many ways the checklist above will help to ensure that people's needs are being met. However, in the early stages when people are reviewing not only their policy but also their actual practice in the school, it might be helpful to consider what is already being done to build relationships in terms of activities and also in terms of skill development. It is also instructive to identify what is currently being done to repair the harm done when relationships are harmed and disconnection has occurred. The blank version of Figure 8.4 in Appendix E can be used as the basis for discussion, adapted to suit the needs of different ages and school roles. The class group, or adult team, can be divided into four groups, with each group being given the task of identifying the current activities/interventions/programmes/lessons where relationships are developed or repaired and write them on a large sheet of paper. The four groups can then assemble their four sheets in the shape of the quadrant shown and perhaps compare their findings with Figure 8.4 in this chapter.

What I have found generally is that lots of excellent relationship and community building activities are already happening. However, the time taken to develop the skills needed to engage effectively in such activities is often consigned to timetabled lessons about PHSE, citizenship or in circle time. This can be asking too much of the teachers responsible for delivering these sessions, which only take up a small percentage of time in any school week. It also would appear to absolve other staff from their responsibility in ensuring that the content of their lessons and teaching style develops these skills.

What usually becomes apparent is that strategies for repairing harm done to relationships and to restoring connectedness are thin on the ground and that often the very concept is new. Many of the skills required to engage in restorative processes are identified as needed by adults first and foremost, who may then feel able to model the skills and help to develop them in the young people.

The exercise can identify the gaps, the need for further development and the areas that need to be considered for developing a whole school approach to relationship. The quadrant itself can serve as a template for developing policy. It can help to identify strategies for prevention of harmful behaviour by promoting pro-social skills and activities, whilst also highlighting strategies and skill development for conflict resolution and restorative approaches.

	RESTORING (Repairing harm done to relationships and community)	RELATING (Developing/nurturing relationships and creating community)
PROCESSES	(a) undisputed responsibility: • Restorative Conferencing • Family Group Conferencing • Victim/Offender Mediation (b) disputed responsibility, conflict, mutual recrimination: • Mediation • Peer Mediation • Family Group Conferencing • Problem-Solving Circles • Restorative Enquiry	Including: • Circle Time for Staff (for planning, review, support and team building) • Circle Time for Students • School Council • Circle of Friends • Peer Counselling and Mentoring • Whole School Development of Relationship Management Policy (cf Behaviour Management, which tends to be student-focused)
SKILLS	**RELATIONSHIPS**	
	skills include: • Nonviolent Communication • Active Non-Judgemental Listening • Conflict Transformation • Developing Empathy and Rapport • Having Difficult Conversations • Restorative Debriefing After Critical Incidents • Understanding and Managing Anger	skills include: • Emotional Literacy • Developing and Maintaining Self-Esteem • Valuing Others Explicitly • Assertiveness • Acknowledging and Appreciating Diversity • Constructively Challenging Oppression and Prejudice • Connecting Across Differences

⬅ **MUCH OVERLAP** ➡

Figure 8.4 Processes and skills involved in restorative/relational justice in schools

Achieving consistency

Having worked in many different schools, primary and secondary, mainstream and special, across the country, I have learnt that what most adults need is a consistent set of guidelines for responding to challenging situations. Dissatisfaction occurs if one person deals with a situation in one way and then another person, often a more senior colleague, deals with it in a different way. I have found that there are two possible scenarios. In the first, what happens is that a distressed classroom teacher or lunchtime controller will refer a young person to someone else because something has happened to damage their relationship with the young person. The person harmed (by an insult, disruptive behaviour or a lack of respect) is angry and distressed, and wants their senior colleague to deal harshly with the young person, thereby demonstrating their solidarity with the aggrieved colleague. In fact, the more senior colleague, who has not had their relationship with the young person damaged, and who is not angry or distressed, is quite likely to 'have a quiet chat' with the young person. He or she calms down, explains what has happened and may even agree, albeit reluctantly, to go and apologise to the aggrieved adult. They do not always get the warm re-acceptance and forgiveness they crave because the aggrieved adult is now not only still angry with the young person but also angry at their colleague for being too soft (Thorsborne 2003).

The second scenario is quite the opposite. In this one the teacher or lunchtime controller may find themselves at their wits' end over the behaviour of a young person. They long for more support but know that if they refer the student to a senior colleague the response will be so heavy handed that their own relationship with the young person could suffer. In neither case is there consistency, and in both cases there is potential for conflict between colleagues and for confusion amongst students.

In fact, once all adults in a school have been trained in the principles and practice of restorative justice, this should go a long way to ensuring consistency across the school. The consistency will lie in the value base underpinning the response and in the intention to repair whatever harm has been caused. Different people will make different judgements about which particular process befits the situation. Pragmatism may play a part in that an intervention is required and there is not enough time to run, say, a full conference with all possible people involved. Nevertheless, whoever deals with a situation, the approach is intent on a similar outcome and the hope is that everyone will feel fairly dealt with.

Restorative practitioners will have at their disposal a set of options, ranging from the empathic listening skills used in restorative enquiry to the highly complex task of facilitating a large group restorative conference. Each school will decide who is the most suitable person to offer these options (see Figure 8.5). Students themselves can be trained to offer many of them, and thus

Response	By?	In response to
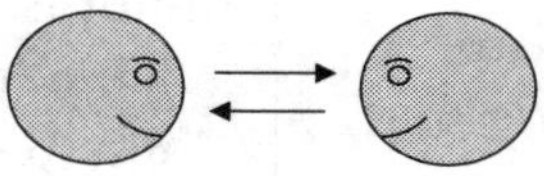 Restorative enquiry	peer mentors teaching staff colleagues	minor student worries minor disruptions need to debrief challenging situations worried parents
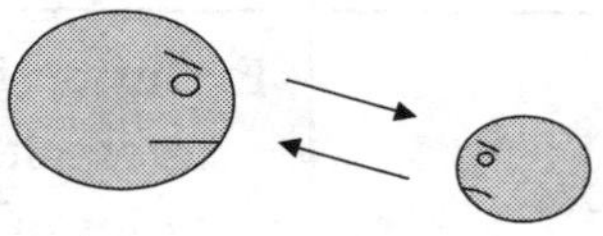 Restorative discussion	teaching staff middle and senior management	disruption causing 'harm' staff disciplinary issues
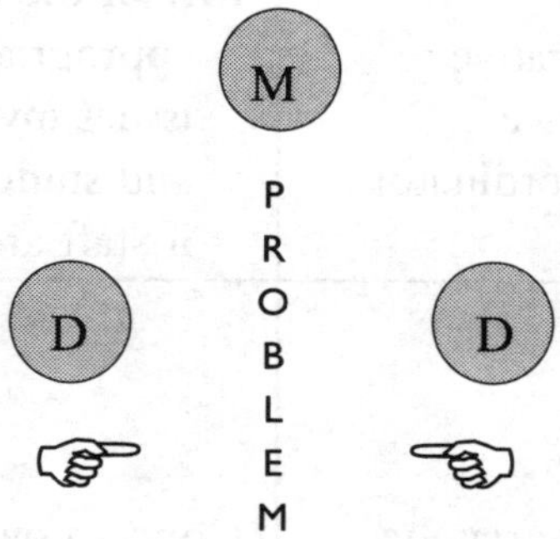 Mediation	peer mediators teaching staff senior managers restorative justice co-ordinator governors/senior management	minor student conflict serious student conflict staff conflict staff–student conflict staff–parent conflict
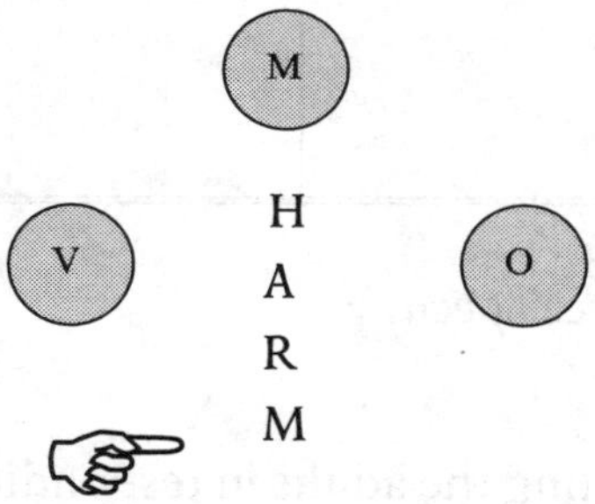 'Victim/Offender' mediation	peer mediators teaching staff senior managers restorative justice co-ordinator governors/senior management	student conflict serious student conflict staff conflict staff–student conflict staff–parent conflict (when there is acknowledged responsibility for the harm caused)
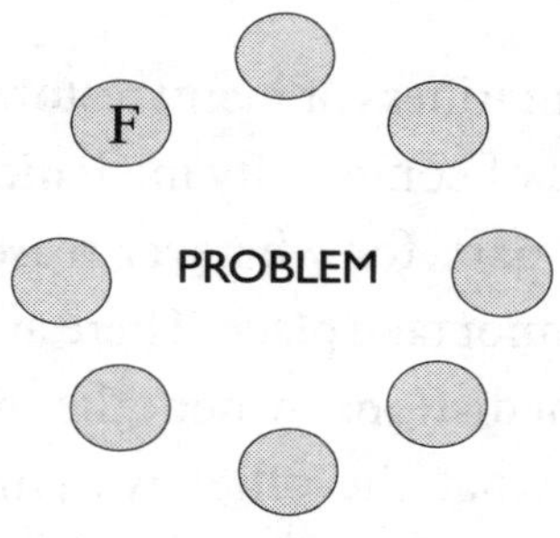 Problem-solving circle	class groups school council whole staff any team staff	class issues/harm within class problems affecting students staff issues team issues

Figure 8.5 The restorative justice options (continued over page)

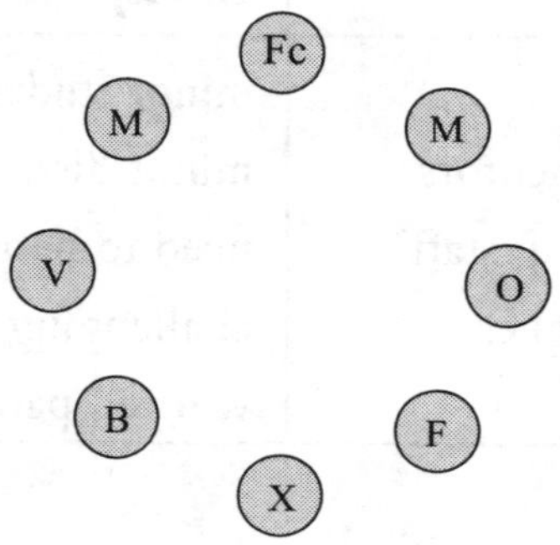

	Peer facilitators	Minor issues involving harm caused in group
	Appropriate teaching staff	Minor issues involving harm/disruption in a group of students
	Senior management	Issues involving a group or needing parental involvement
Restorative conference	Governors	Exclusion issues – either as an alternative, or at point of re-entry to school
	Restorative justice co-ordinator	Any of the above if appropriate, and also issues involving staff and students (especially if staff are 'offenders')
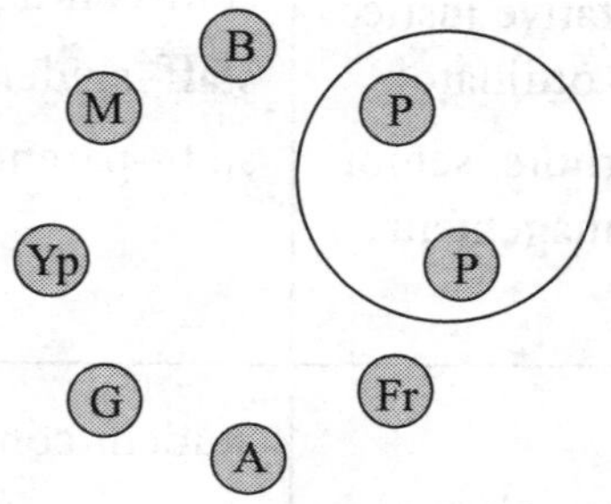 Family group conference	Appropriately trained facilitators	Concern over a students' situation or behaviour e.g. attendance, at risk

Figure 8.5 (continued) The restorative justice options

extend their own skills whilst supporting the adults in responding to challenges as they occur.

Voluntariness

A lot of emphasis is placed on the voluntariness of many restorative processes in the criminal justice field and in the field of community mediation. In these fields if any one side does not want to take part, for whatever reason, then a direct face-to-face restorative intervention cannot take place. There are various options including what are called shuttle mediations, when the mediators act as go-betweens, relaying to each party what the other is saying. Clearly, in a situation involving a lot of people, this could become unwieldy and confusing.

A school will need to decide to what extent its restorative processes are voluntary. It is certainly true that one cannot force someone to come to a meeting, and threats of punishment or disciplinary action in the event of refusal to turn up would be preposterous in such a situation. Nevertheless, if a young person, a parent or a member of staff were not prepared to engage in this way there would need to be alternative responses available. The question is whether these alternatives can still be restorative or whether they need to be retributive. The main points to consider would be:

- What strategies are available for responding to unacceptable behaviour if the person responsible will not meet with those he or she has affected by their behaviour?

- What strategies are available for working with those who have been harmed by unacceptable behaviour if these people will not meet those who have harmed them?

- What strategies can be used when the various parties in a conflict do not want to meet?

- What strategies are available even if all sides are happy to meet but there is no time to arrange such a meeting?

- What restorative strategies can be used by people when the person they are addressing appears to not want to listen, let alone respond?

- Is the school going to have a two-pronged approach, in which those who agree to take part in a restorative process may do so, whilst those who will not will be sanctioned?

- If sanctions remain the alternative with the unwilling, will these also be applicable to adults and is that built into the internal discipline procedures of the school? Would such a scheme be acceptable to the teaching unions?

- Are there any behaviours that do not merit a restorative response?

Such issues raise a lot of questions. My sense is that using retributive approaches as an alternative to a restorative approach carries the risk of being very undemocratic. I cannot see the teaching unions allowing their members to be sanctioned for refusing to take part in a restorative, process and quite rightly so. Coercion in an essentially uncoercive approach would be highly inappropriate and flies in the face of a restorative value base. Considering the issue from the perspective of an adult highlights the absurdity of sanctioning a young person for opting out. It would be extremely undemocratic to have one response for an unwilling student and another response for an unwilling adult. People are likely to be unwilling for a variety of reasons, and it may be that identifying what people need in order to participate is the key.

However, whatever one does there may always be people who will not engage and do not appear interested in reconnecting with those around them.

This leaves the issue of how a school will address such situations. My suggestion is that this issue is discussed by the school community at the outset of the project. The young people are likely to have strong views about what they find helps when they behave in ways that are out of order. They may come up with a continuum of responses based on experience. The point is that very few young people share the prevalent adult view that sanctions teach them to change their ways. They have a lot to teach us in this respect.

Similarly the adults in a school community may need to air their own concerns about engaging in restorative processes. A sense of exposure and vulnerability is a common reason for their reluctance. Fear of loss of face, loss of authority and loss of respect are all fears that need to be addressed. What is at stake is the very nature of the adult–student relationship, and restorative projects are inviting the whole school community to reconsider what this relationship might be.

Whatever responses are developed, they need to be underpinned by the restorative values already highlighted and draw on the restorative skills already described in this book. Inappropriate behaviour and a reluctance to engage does not mean that an individual is unworthy of respect, support or reconnection.

Summary

This chapter has discussed the importance of relationships in a school community. It has made a case for developing a relationship management policy rather than a behaviour management policy, which is so often predicated on rewards and sanctions, and tends to focus on the behaviour of only one constituency of the community – the young people. It has argued that punitive responses to harmful behaviour neither meet the needs of those engaging in such behaviour nor achieve the hoped-for outcomes of those responding in this way. It has stressed the importance of connectedness in helping young people feel safe and its role in reducing anti-social and destructive behaviour. It has argued for a response to harmful behaviour that seeks to reconnect those who have been disconnected by such behaviour and has highlighted this need for all ages across the school community. The importance of ensuring that a relationship management policy is underpinned by restorative values is emphasised, as is the need to involve the whole school community in shaping the policy. Finally the chapter has given some practical suggestions to help a school community engage in an exploration of how to ensure a consistency of intention across the school.

The next chapter provides evidence from recent evaluations of restorative projects of the importance of consistency, and provides a model of school change that will help people embark on the first steps.

Chapter 9
Piecing Together the Jigsaw

> Restorative approaches in schools provide a means of redistributing power along more equitable lines.
>
> Secondary School-based Youth Worker

The message of this book is that ultimately a restorative project will be much more effective if it is part of a whole school approach, in which everyone in the school community is using restorative skills on a daily basis. This is certainly the message from evaluations of initiatives involving what I have described as a restorative ethos, such as circle time and peer mediation. It is also reflected in the recommendations from early evaluation of current restorative projects in schools. This chapter refers to some of this evaluation in more detail, considers some of the messages from the literature of school improvement, and also draws inspiration from some international school initiatives.

The chapter acknowledges that embarking on wholesale organisational change from the very outset is daunting and may well prevent some schools from taking that first step. It considers ways of making a start and takes a realistic view of timescales and expectations.

Finally, the chapter offers a challenge to the Department for Education and Skills, the Teacher Training Agency and the government to see the links between the initiatives they are already developing in education and those in the criminal justice arena.

Involving the whole school

In recent years a variety of techniques and strategies have been introduced into schools that contribute to the building and repairing of relationships within a school. These include circle time, described more fully in Chapter 7, and peer mediation, briefly described in Chapter 5. Even more recently, several new restorative conferencing initiatives have been introduced into schools. Many of these projects have been evaluated, and the feedback has relevance for anyone about to embark on a restorative project.

In her assessment of the success of circle time, Hilary Cremin, from Oxford Brookes University, identifies several reasons why circle time is often neglected or ineffective (Cremin 2002a), two of which are particularly pertinent to developing a restorative approach. The first is what Cremin describes as societal attitudes towards power, control and children, and the expectation on teachers to coerce and control their students – an expectation shared by many teachers themselves. She highlights a tension between the egalitarian facilitative style of teaching required in running a circle time session and the more authoritarian style of some teachers.

> Teachers are nearly always kind, well-meaning and professional, but for children to be truly empowered schools would need to be places in which the values of tolerance, acceptance, creative problem-solving and self awareness (adults and children) extended beyond Circle Time. (Cremin 2002a, p.26)

Second, without a whole school, developmental approach to PHSE and circle time, the values and attitudes encouraged in these sessions are much less likely to flourish. Cremin argues for the integration of the values of circle time into all curriculum areas, as well as opportunities to use the skills developed in circle time sessions such as active listening, co-operation and negotiating.

In an earlier article about peer mediation, an area in which she has had extensive experience as a trainer, a consultant and a researcher, Cremin highlights certain essential features for the success of the project, including: pupil empowerment; a whole school approach; resources; support of mediators; training in effective conflict resolution for the whole school community and the support of senior management (Cremin 2002b). Elsewhere she has argued that attitudinal change on the part of adults is a crucial key to the success of mediation:

> In my experience children make wonderful mediators. It is invariably adults who need to review their attitudes towards conflict, power and control if peer mediation in a school setting is to thrive. (Cremin 2000, p.142)

This message comes across clearly in the report of a peer mediation project in south London, which states:

> If there is a weak link in the conflict resolution framework…it is the fact that there is no consistent whole school approach to conflict. Different members of staff deal with student–student conflict in different ways. (Bitel and Rolls 2000, p.79)

Jerry Tyrrell, whose work developing peer mediation in Northern Ireland is described in a book that was published after his death in 2001 (Tyrrell 2002), warns against an agenda of 'negative peacemaking' in which the prime motivation for developing a peer mediation scheme is to ensure children behave properly, as opposed to giving them conflict management skills and providing them with opportunities for using these skills.

The CRISP (Crime Reduction in Schools Project) initiative in Leicester advocates working only in schools that have an open culture in which adults are willing to nurture student responsibility, and that have featured conflict management and dispute resolution in their development plan and their curriculum. The managers of this project are also very keen to stress the active involvement of students and staff in the development of their own project, so that it meets their own 'unique and individual needs' (Griffiths 2003).

Common themes emerge from these reflections on circle time and peer mediation and the importance of bringing everyone on board, especially the teaching staff, is continually referred to.

It is not surprising to find that similar conclusions are being made by early evaluations of restorative projects. One report of restorative projects in the Thames Valley refers to a school's 'readiness' for a project, in terms of its receptiveness to restorative values and principles. It also emphasises how important the role of the senior management and the governors will be in providing the time for awareness raising, training practice, ongoing support and implementation (Preston 2002).

In their final report on a restorative justice pilot project in Lambeth schools, begun in the summer of 2000, the evaluators make 11 recommendations, the third of which endorses everything already said about involving the whole school:

> Restorative justice conference programmes need a whole-school commitment. Whole-school restorative justice approaches require the following components:
>
> ○ there needs to be sufficient teacher training time so that the majority of teachers are familiar with the intervention before implementation begins
>
> ○ any teacher who desires to be trained as a facilitator should be given the opportunity to do so
>
> ○ in addition, schools need to design ways by which information about the conference process can be conveyed to all students
>
> ○ the option of the restorative justice conference must be included explicitly in the school's behaviour policy. (Edgar *et al.* 2002, p.*vii*)

This last point is elaborated by a concession that there may be room for some punitive responses in a restorative whole school approach, but it is recommended that such responses do not intrude into the restorative conference process. My own perspective has been rehearsed in previous chapters, but it is useful to know that there are other views on this, and ultimately pragmatism will teach us what can be achieved.

International examples of the whole school approach

The concept of running a school along restorative lines would appear to be relatively new in the UK, and evaluation is at an early stage. Experiences from the United States provide useful pointers to the way forward, however. In Pennsylvania there are six schools or day programmes run along restorative lines by not-for-profit organisation Community Safety Foundation (CSF) Buxmont Academy. Their work with youth at risk has shown substantial evidence that living and working in a restorative environment can make a big impact on the behaviour and attitudes of the young people (McCold 2002). In these schools there is great emphasis put on student–student, staff–student and staff–staff relationships, so that what is created is a 'restorative milieu'.

> Within this restorative milieu, youth are held accountable for their actions while being given the social and emotional support necessary to make changes. Restorative practices empower the young person and the group to develop their own behavioural standards and actively confront misbehaviour. The young people act as a micro-community for each other, consciously building interdependency and a sense of responsibility to the community. This process is facilitated by CSF Buxmont staff. (McCold 2002)

Clearly restorative practices are integrated into the school day and everyone feels involved and accountable. Early reports from a new CSF school in Hungary suggest that the gains are also tangible for the adults in the school, where mutual support is a workplace priority (Mirsky 2002).

Supporting whole school change

It is clear from the preceding sections that the involvement of the whole school community, and the integration of restorative practices into the daily activities of the school community, are both crucial for a restorative project to succeed. Evaluation reports and recommendations agree on this. However, evidence of effective whole school culture change is less readily available.

Research into the fast-growing literature on school change would seem to endorse a restorative approach to change – one that emphasises mutual respect, inclusion, listening to the needs, feelings and opinions of everyone involved, flexibility and setting realistic, achievable goals.

Andy Hargreaves and Michael Fullan, two of the 'gurus' of school change, distinguish between 'restructuring' a school, which involves formal changes to timetables, roles and organisation, and 'reculturing' a school, which 'involves changing the norms, values, incentives, skills, and relationships in an organisation to support (and prod) people to work differently together' (Hargreaves and Fullan 1998, p.128). In their experience the former, 'restructuring', does little to improve teaching and learning, whereas the latter, 'reculturing', certainly does.

Restructuring will need to be a part of reculturing, but Hargreaves and Fullan emphasise that the structural changes come about after the school community has invested emotionally in 'transforming the culture and relationships in a school over many years' (Hargreaves and Fullan 1998, p.129). The structural changes then come from within, identified by everyone as important to enhance the cultural and relationship changes that have been made.

A five-stage model of change

Bearing in mind the need for whole school involvement, and the importance of a change process which is underpinned by restorative values, what is proposed is a five-stage model (see Table 9.1). This model advocates involvement and consultation with every member of the school community from the outset, and allows for ongoing representation throughout the life of the project. In its conception it allows for flexibility and ownership by the school itself. No two

	Table 9.1 A five-stage model for school change along restorative lines
Stage 1	Owning and developing the vision: Awareness-raising sessions and a chance for everyone in the school to ask questions and make suggestions. Some baseline evaluation of school climate might be worthwhile at this stage so change can be measured.
Stage 2	Establishing and developing a steering group, involving representatives from across the school community. This group is responsible for the development, the monitoring and the oversight of the project. They will need basic training in restorative approaches at the outset so the project is managed restoratively.
Stage 3	Identifying and establishing the training team from within the school, also using representation from across the school community. This team will need basic training in the skills and then training for trainers.
Stage 4	Developing and supporting the training team as the training begins across the school, with lunchtime teams, class groups, curriculum and year teams, governors, parents (or whoever the steering group has identified as a target group).
Stage 5	Policy and organisational review to ensure restorative practice and ethos is integrated into every aspect of the school day.

schools are likely to interpret the model in the same way, but it provides a structure on which to base the project.

The first stage

The initial awareness-raising proposed in Stage 1 might follow the approach suggested in Chapter 2 of this book. The ways forward will vary for each school, but ensuring opportunities for communication, and developing the listening skills of the whole school community along the lines of Chapter 3, will be important starting points. Following some initial introductory sessions about the whole school restorative approach to teaching staff, governors, parents, students and ancillary staff (and every other group that has an interest in the school and its well-being), time needs to be made for ongoing discussion.

There is no reason to postpone all new initiatives until Stages 4 and 5. If the initial ideas inspire the various constituencies to keep talking amongst themselves, then the use of circles can begin almost at once, as described in Chapter 7. Relational and restorative circles at the start of a school day, for every class and every staff team, could be a rapid way to transform the culture of classrooms and staff rooms. This is not unattainable. Some schools are already making time for these circle meetings, and finding them a lifeline for getting through the school day. Longer meetings once a week could then follow up issues of a more complex nature, or allow for some more team building through celebration, fun and games. The only caveat is that skilled circle facilitators amongst staff and students will be needed to ensure everyone benefits from the meetings. The preparation for this task need not be lengthy, however, and might be a priority in the early days.

This first stage of initial awareness-raising need only take a few weeks whilst the benefit of beginning almost at once by introducing time for circles creates a sense of excitement and progress.

The second stage

It is vital that the steering group is made up of representatives from across the school community, who have opportunities to report back to their 'constituents'. Thus a group might include:

- the headteacher
- the member of senior management with pastoral responsibility
- a school governor
- parent representatives from different year groups
- year heads
- member of staff responsible for PHSE and citizenship

- members of the school council

- representative from ancillary staff

- representative from lunchtime staff

- representative from administrative staff

- representative from the behaviour support team

- representative from the catering staff/maintenance team.

The group will become unwieldy and the meetings difficult to co-ordinate if numbers are too high, but by the same token failure to hear any particular voice could lead to conflict. The group would need to agree how those unable to attend will remain informed and have their say. It will also need to be considered how each representative can remain in touch with those they are representing, so there are opportunities for a two-way flow of information and views.

Suggestions for feedback include a regular project newsletter; school council meetings and assemblies; time taken in staff/team/year and senior management meetings for recent updates of progress and a chance to raise questions; a small library of relevant magazines, newspaper cuttings, books and videos on different restorative processes to help people inform themselves.

The steering group would be the first cohort within the school to be trained in restorative processes. The group would need this training to understand the full extent of what is possible, to be able to run all their meetings along restorative lines and to become advocates for the approach with their peers. Early on, they would establish achievable, measurable goals and ensure that evaluation was built in to every stage. This evaluation would be of both a quantitative and a qualitative nature, to measure changes not just in behaviour but also in attitudes and perceptions.

In projects I am currently involved in we have used the paradigm shift questionnaire in Figure 8.3 to get some idea of where teacher thinking is at the outset of a project, and then used it again after the initial training. It could be used along the way as well to measure changes in teacher thinking and behaviour. As Fullan says: 'Educational change depends on what teachers do and think – it's as simple and as complex as that' (Fullan 1991, p.117). I am advocating that cultural change depends on what everyone does and thinks, but the point is worth remembering. If teachers are not on board, fully supported as they relinquish old habits and learn new ones, the project will flounder.

A simple questionnaire for school students can help involve them in thinking about school safety and climate. One school in Wendover in Buckinghamshire involved the students themselves in designing a questionnaire that was then answered by staff and students alike. This would certainly be demonstrating respect for the students' views on what is important to find out and what is worth measuring. It would also ensure that the questionnaire was written in accessible language.

The group would meet regularly to monitor ongoing developments and would be identifying where and when certain initiatives will be taken.

The second and third stages are innovative and empowering. They provide the exit strategy that any external change agent needs to ensure the long-term survival of a project. They also provide capacity to an internally driven project to ensure that the responsibility for implementation and ongoing support does not rest on too few pairs of shoulders.

The second stage could take some time, depending on how often and for how long the group meets. I would recommend that once the first stage has established a commitment to the project the initial training of the steering group happens very quickly. People need to experience restorative practices for themselves, and then they will understand their potential. After that there will be a sense of urgency to start to roll this approach out in the school. Deciding exactly where to start, and how this will happen, may take a while, but the third stage can be happening simultaneously.

If a school has the enthusiasm and commitment I would expect the training of both the steering group and the in-house training team to be completed in a term.

The third stage

A steering group trained in restorative skills, and experienced in pioneering the change process, would develop capacity within the school to anticipate and overcome the challenges as they occur. A training team made up of representatives from across the school community, trained not only in restorative skills but also in the training skills to roll out the programme to others, ensures that the project has a future as students and teachers move on to other schools.

Several peer mediation programmes in Berkshire regularly invite new mediators onto their team and they are trained by the existing mediators in their weekly support meetings until such time as they feel skilled enough to go on the rota.

The fourth stage

The fourth stage can begin once the trainers feel confident that they are ready to train their peers or colleagues in restorative skills. The starting points will have been identified by the steering group, in consultation with key representatives for the rest of the school.

Examples of ways in which schools are introducing restorative practices include:

- introducing circle time into tutor/classroom time for all students so they can develop communities of support for each other whilst also helping each other become accountable for the impact of their behaviour on each other

- using circles with staff and with parent groups for the same reasons

- training students to be either peer mentors, who are trained in restorative enquiry (Chapter 3), or peer mediators, whose training goes a stage further so they can mediate the conflicts of their fellow students (Chapter 5)

- introducing conflict management and emotional literacy skills into the curriculum through PHSE and citizenship; these are briefly described in Chapter 4 and there is an increasing literature on these subjects, with plenty of useful classroom materials

- using restorative conferencing and mediation to address misbehaviour and bullying to avoid the need for exclusion and further disconnection

- training key staff in restorative skills so they can cascade to their colleagues new ways of dealing with day-to-day challenging situations in school.

Time for training will always be at a premium, but a skilled team will identify ways of integrating skills development into the curriculum and into departmental, curriculum, staff and team meetings that are held regularly anyway. The most powerful way to learn is by example, so that many of the approaches will be picked up by observation of more experienced practitioners. This has certainly been the story told to me by some teachers in schools where more senior colleagues are already running restorative conferences, for example.

Once there are skilled practitioners in a school community, ongoing training can be done either through timetabled, organised courses or by 'sitting by Nelly' – a wonderful phrase to describe learning by observing skilled practitioners at work. In fact, the ideal situation could be an initial introduction followed by mentoring and support by those with more experience.

The training team might be offering, at any given time, training in:

- circle time facilitation (see Chapter 7)

- community circle facilitation (problem-solving circles in Chapter 7)

- peer mentoring skills

- peer mediation skills

- restorative conferencing and mediation skills for adults

- conflict management for students

- conflict management for adults.

They may also be offering refresher courses and supervision meetings for any of the above.

The time frame for this is impossible to predict because it depends on timetable commitments and the need for other initiatives to be developing alongside. Teaching staff have only so many hours they can commit to after-school training and meetings, and students may not want to give up precious relaxation time in breaks.

However, it will become clear to everyone involved that all of the skills above are vital life skills. Competence in such skills will also develop the self-esteem, articulacy, confidence and assertiveness of everyone who engages in the training. They will enhance everyone's awareness of each other, heightening compassion, respect and responsibility within the school community.

It is early days to point to statistics, but anecdotal evidence suggests that such training will impact not only on all of the above but will also create a more effective teaching and learning environment and thus improve academic results. In other words, the whole school community may be happy to make that extra effort in order to create a better environment for one another.

The fifth stage

The final stage is not really a stage but an ongoing process that will be needed to keep the approach alive and well. The following list of key performance indicators would need to be ever-present in the minds of those responsible for the project:

- the ongoing commitment of senior managers and governors to the approach

- liaison with multi-agency staff beyond the school community who support the wider community and the young people at risk (e.g. social services, educational support services, police)

- ongoing induction and skills development of new staff and students

- someone to take responsibility for the preparation of more complex restorative interventions, where necessary, and for ensuring the necessary follow-up support is carried out

- ongoing record-keeping and evaluation of restorative interventions and their impact on the individuals involved, and the wider community

- liaison with colleagues responsible for curriculum areas where the development of relational and restorative skills play an important part (e.g. PHSE and citizenship)

- keeping abreast of initiatives and training opportunities in the field locally and nationally

- liaison with other restorative justice co-ordinators locally and nationally

- identification of links between restorative practices and other key policy areas of the school, not least the policies on behaviour and relationship management of the school, teaching and learning, equal opportunities, self-esteem and special educational needs.

Ideally, a restorative project will be supported and sustained by a team of people, but once the whole school culture has been imbued with restorative principles it may be that the everyday management of the approach is left to an individual – the restorative justice co-ordinator.

The restorative justice co-ordinator

Every school should have one. It would be my dream that in a few years' time the *Times Educational Supplement*, a weekly publication read by most teachers in the UK, would include a section for restorative justice co-ordinators. The job description of this person would not be to effect whole school change. It should be clear from the previous discussion that many more people are needed for that complex process. The key performance indicators listed above may form a large part of their role, but it is clear that these need to be addressed in consultation with many others.

A supporting curriculum for teachers and students

Just as the ideal scenario would be for every school to have its own full-time restorative justice co-ordinator, so, in the future, it would make sense to build relational and restorative skills into the curriculum of students and trainee teachers alike.

At the moment there is scope for school students to have these opportunities in their PHSE and citizenship lessons, and during circle time, if they are lucky to have this on a regular basis. However, provision is sporadic, not every course provides these opportunities and not every teacher is trained to provide them in an experiential, participative way. In secondary schools there is often plenty of opportunity for team building and circle time during tutorial slots. What is needed are more circle facilitators. Chapters 7 and 8 have already indicated that facilitating a circle can be a challenge for someone who is unwilling or unable to relinquish control of the process. Some training in, and understanding of, key restorative principles is needed.

It becomes very clear that what is vitally and urgently needed is a review of initial teacher training. Why, when many teachers are crying out for it, and when so much research emphasises the importance of good relationships for effective learning (Brighouse and Woods 2000; Docking 2002; MacGilchrist, Myers and

Reed 1997), is so little time given to the relational and restorative aspects of good teaching? Enthusiastic schools can only do so much. For long-term change, initiatives need to come from the Department for Educational and Skills and from the Teacher Training Agency. Curriculum change is only one such initiative, however. Just as significant is a shift in priorities.

The challenge of time and conflicting priorities

As long as adults in schools, and the parents of the school students, feel pressurised to meet the Standards Agenda currently set by the government, long-term systemic uptake of restorative approaches is less likely. Many teachers say, during training sessions, that whatever the ideal response, it is not always possible to take the time required for a fully restorative response. Teachers' performance is measured on their test and examination results, not on the extent to which they are kind, caring human beings, developing the rounded personalities of their students. Ironically, research suggests that in fact the key to effective teaching lies in combining being kind, caring and attentive to the whole young person, together with effective classroom management skills and teaching techniques.

Whether or not people have the time to respond with time and a listening ear, we cannot get away from the fact that most behaviour management systems fail to address consistently the underlying needs of those who are behaving in challenging ways, fail to prevent the very behaviours they are addressing and fail to achieve the outcomes they set out to fulfil. Furthermore, they often create more harm than good by damaging the relationships and connections between the students themselves and between students and the adults who work with them. As mentioned in Chapter 8, a disconnected student will not work at their best.

It is no doubt true that teachers are often under too much pressure to deliver academic results to take the time to respond to unmet needs appropriately and to spend time on developing pro-social skills. Once again it is worth stating forcefully that schools will need support if they want to change their culture from retributive to restorative, and to become a listening school where students and adults want to spend their working week. They will need this support and encouragement from the local education authority and more importantly from the Department for Education and Skills. I have alluded earlier to the tension between trying to meet the Standards Agenda as well as the Inclusion Agenda.

As I write, the Home Office is becoming increasingly enthusiastic about restorative justice. Through the Youth Justice Board it is sponsoring several Restorative Justice in Schools projects, as well as developing restorative approaches to offending behaviour by the youth offending teams. It is hoped that soon the government will appreciate what this support might entail for schools to develop their restorative policies. The Department for Education and Skills, the

Teacher Training Agency and OFSTED all have a vital role in supporting schools to develop good practice by shifting priorities. In fact, effective teaching and learning depends on good relationships. Behaving in a pro-social way develops from understanding and a sense of community and collective responsibility. Restorative values, skills and practices will ensure that the government can achieve high standards as well as create inclusive school communities.

Summary

In this chapter the whole school approach advocated by the whole book has been set in the context of ongoing research and evaluation of related school improvement projects. The chapter has referred to the need for whole school involvement, and to a congruence of approach throughout the school community. It has given a practical model of school change that is inspired by restorative principles, whilst also reflecting many ideas from the literature and research in this field.

There are an increasing number of restorative projects being developed in schools around the world, and we all have much to learn from each other. This chapter has referred to just two of them. However, inspiration for this book has come from the wider international restorative community and its support and encouragement has been acknowledged throughout the book where appropriate. The ideas discussed in this book are part of the exciting blossoming of restorative practice in schools all over the world, and another book is needed to tell that big story.

I have chosen to set this book almost exclusively in the context of the UK and make reference to schools I know and to my own experiences. I hope this brings to it a fresh flavour and a practical feel. These are exciting times. Despite the sharp words about government policy, I know there are people in high places who want to make changes. I have already referred to the remark of Keith Bradley, Home Office minister, made at the launch of one restorative justice project in 2000:

'Restorative justice is an idea whose time has come.'

I believe it is definitely an idea whose time has come in schools, and I hope this book will inspire and enable many people to turn the idea into a reality.

Appendix A

Restorative Enquiry

Restorative Enquiry: The Past

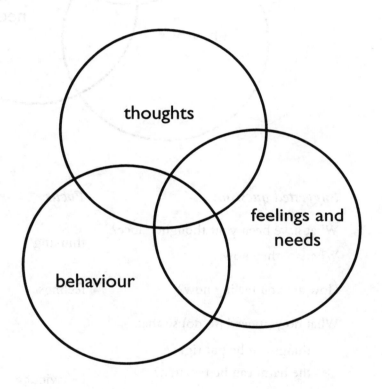

Suggested question	Focus
Can you explain what happened?	thinking (interpretation) and behaviour
What were you thinking at the time?	thinking
How were you feeling at the time?	feelings
Who else do you think has been affected by this?	others' feelings, thoughts and behaviours

Restorative Enquiry: The Present and Future

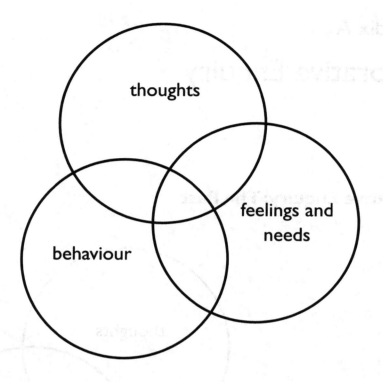

Suggested question	Focus
What have been your thoughts since? What are they now?	thinking
How are you feeling now?	feelings
What do you need (to do) so that: • things can be put right? • the harm can be repaired? • you can move on? (This question can be adapted to suit the context.)	behaviour

Appendix B

Restorative Enquiry Adapted for a Conference

Stage 2 – Hearing the Stories

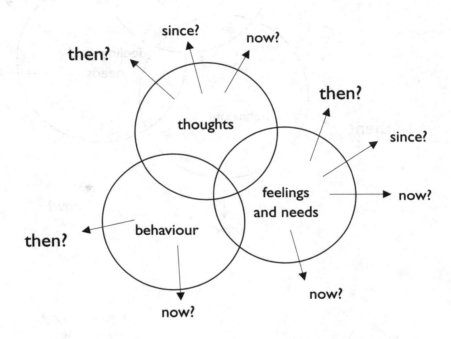

Suggested question	Focus
Can you explain what happened?	thinking (interpretation) and behaviour
What were you thinking at the time?	thinking
How were you feeling at the time?	feelings
What have been your thoughts since?	thinking
What are they now?	thinking
How are you feeling now?	feelings
Who else do you think has been affected by this?	others' feelings, thoughts and behaviours

Stage 3 – Moving Forward

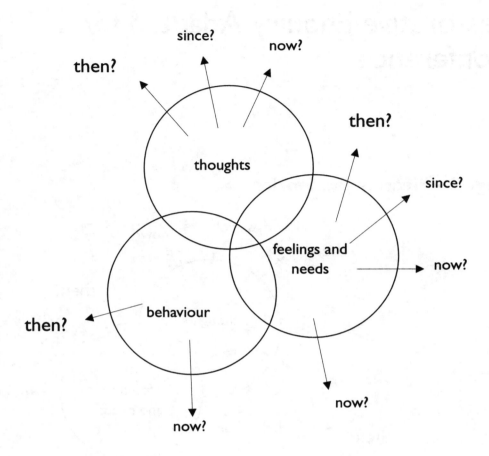

Suggested question

What do you need (to do) so that:

- things can be put right?
- the harm can be repaired?
- you can move on?

Focus

behaviour

© Belinda Hopkins 2004

Stage 4 – Clarifying the Agreement

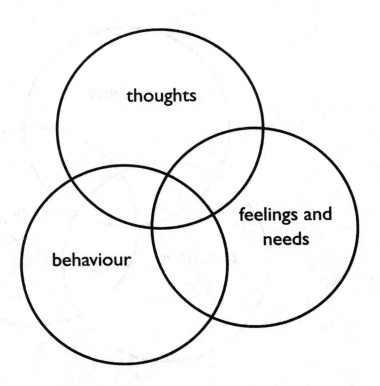

Suggested question	Focus
What do you think about X's suggestion?	thinking/feelings
What else would you need/to do?	needs
When/how/where will this happen?	behaviour
Would you like this written down?	needs

Stage 5 – Recognition, Rehabilitation and Closure

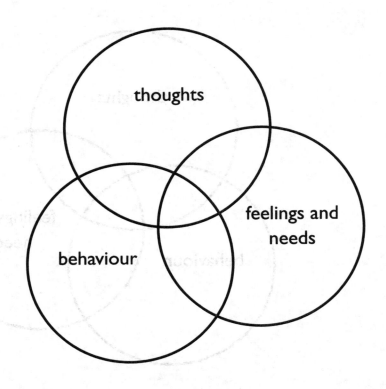

Suggested question	Focus
How can this situation be dealt with differently another time?	thinking
How are you feeling?	feelings
Is there anything else you would like to say to anyone here?	behaviour

Appendix C

Self-Review Questionnaires

Self-Review Questionnaire for Senior Management

	Yes	No	Not Sure
Am I approachable?	☐	☐	☐
Do people feel safe to talk to me about their concerns?	☐	☐	☐
Do I ensure that there are no interruptions wherever possible?	☐	☐	☐
Do I appear interested in what people are saying?	☐	☐	☐
Do I listen in a respectful way?	☐	☐	☐
Do I acknowledge their feelings?	☐	☐	☐
Do I let people finish what they need to say before I respond?	☐	☐	☐
Do I check with people what kind of response they need from me?	☐	☐	☐
Do I respect people's views even when I don't agree with them?	☐	☐	☐
After talking to me do people feel heard?	☐	☐	☐
How do I know the answers to all of the above?	☐	☐	☐
Have I asked people, or am I making assumptions?	☐	☐	☐

Self-Review Questionnaire for teaching staff, lunchtime staff and classroom assistants

	Yes	No	Not Sure
Do I respect young people's feelings even when I might think an issue is trivial?	☐	☐	☐
Do I encourage my students to resolve their own problems rather than provide solutions?	☐	☐	☐
Does this encouragement nevertheless convey care and concern?	☐	☐	☐
If I am in conflict with a student, colleague or parent do I invite them to give me their perspective before passing judgement?	☐	☐	☐
Do I try and understand the reasons behind people's behaviour?	☐	☐	☐
Do I think of myself as a good listener?	☐	☐	☐
How do I know?	☐	☐	☐

Self-Review Questionnaire for Office Staff

	Yes	No	Not Sure
Do I greet everyone, including students, with a smile?	☐	☐	☐
Is my telephone manner warm and helpful?	☐	☐	☐
Do I acknowledge people, even if I am on the phone when they arrive?	☐	☐	☐
Do I help people to feel welcome even when I am busy?	☐	☐	☐
Do I find out what people need in an encouraging way?	☐	☐	☐

Self-Review Questionnaire for Catering Staff

	Yes	No	Not Sure
Do I greet customers warmly, whether they are students, teachers or visitors?	☐	☐	☐
Do people feel safe to ask me about the choices that day?	☐	☐	☐
Do I acknowledge polite behaviour as much as, or more than, I comment on discourtesy in the dinner queue?	☐	☐	☐
Am I patient with young people struggling with choosing food or finding the correct money?	☐	☐	☐

Appendix D

Checklist for a Relationship Management Policy

Is the policy underpinned by the following values?

- Mutual respect ☐
- Trust ☐
- Openness ☐
- Empowerment ☐
- Connectedness ☐
- Tolerance ☐
- Integrity ☐
- Conguence ☐
- People have the need and ability to resolve their own problems ☐
- Acceptance of diverse experience and points of view ☐
- Valuing one another ☐
- Acknowledgement ☐
- Encouragement ☐
- Listening ☐
- Sharing ideas ☐
- Acceptance that mistakes happen and we learn from them ☐
- Importance of feelings, needs and rights ☐

Restorative/Relational Justice in Schools

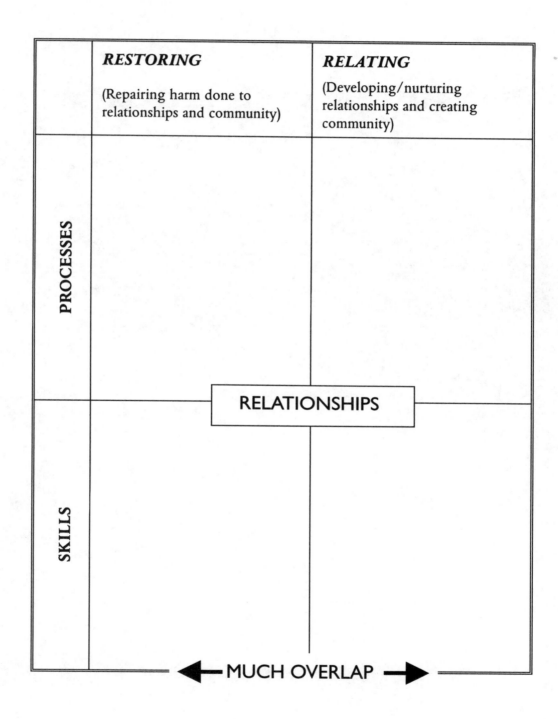

References

APPGC (2002) *Commitment to Children.* London: All Party Parliamentary Group for Children Review.

AVP (1986) *Alternatives to Violence Project Basic Course Manual.* New York: Alternatives to Violence Project.

Bentley, C., Bentley, M., Conchie, J., Liebmann, M., Musgrave, R. and Williams, P. (1998) *Mediation Works.* Bristol: Mediation UK.

Bitel, M. and Rolls, D. (2000) 'Mediation in a South London Secondary School.' In M. Liebmann (ed) *Mediation in Context.* London: Jessica Kingsley Publishers.

Bliss, T.G., Robinson, G. and Maines, B. (1995) *Developing Circle Time.* Bristol: Lucky Duck Publishing.

Blood, P. (2000) Personal communication.

Boserup, H. (2002) 'Keeping Up with the Latest Model.' *Mediation Matters 71,* 12–14.

Braithwaite, J. (1989) *Crime, Shame and Reintegration.* Cambridge: Cambridge University Press.

Brighouse, T. and Woods, T. (2000) *How to Improve Your School.* London: Routledge/Falmer.

Brouwers, A. and Tomic, W. (2000) 'A Longitudinal Study of Teacher Burnout and Perceived Self-efficacy in Classroom Management.' *Teaching and Teacher Education 16,* 239–253.

Bush, R. and Folger, J. (1994) *The Promise of Mediation.* San Francisco: Jossey-Bass.

Cameron, L. and Thorsborne, M. (2001) 'Restorative Justice and School Discipline – Mutually Exclusive?' In H. Strang and J. Braithwaite (eds) *Restorative Justice and Civil Society.* Cambridge: Cambridge University Press.

Cloke, K. and Goldsmith, J. (2000) *Resolving Personal and Organizational Conflict.* San Francisco: Jossey-Bass.

Coates, R. and Gehm, J. (1989) 'An Empirical Assessment.' In M. Wright and B. Galaway (eds) *Mediation and Criminal Justice.* London: Sage.

Cornelius, H. and Faire, S. (1993) *Everyone Can Win.* East Roseville, NSW: Simon and Schuster.

Crawley, J. (1995) *Training Manual in Community Mediation Skills*. Bristol: Mediation UK.

Cremin, H. (2000) 'School Mediation Works.' *Mediation 63*, 7.

Cremin, H. (2002a) 'Circle Time: Why It Doesn't Always Work.' *Primary Practice 30*, 23–29.

Cremin, H. (2002b) 'Pupils Resolving Disputes: Successful Peer Mediation Schemes Share Their Secrets.' *Support for Learning 17*, 138–142.

Cremin, H. (2002c) Personal communication.

Davis, G. (1992) *Making Amends: Mediation and Reparation in Criminal Justice*. London: Routledge.

Dignan, J. (2002) 'Reparation Orders.' In B. Williams (ed) *Reparation and Victim-Focused Social Work*. London: Jessica Kingsley Publishers.

Docking, J. (2002) *Managing Behaviour in the Primary School*. London: David Fulton Publishers.

Edgar, K., Bitel, M., Thurlow, J. and Bowen, G. (2002) *The Evaluation of the Lambeth Restorative Justice Conference Pilot Project in Schools*. Oxford: Partners in Evaluation and the Centre for Criminological Research, Oxford University.

Faber, A. and Mazlish, E. (1980) *How to Talk So Kids Will Listen and Listen So Kids Will Talk*. New York: Rawson/Wade Publishers.

Farrington, L. (2000) *Playground Peacemakers*. Plymouth: Loxley Enterprises.

Fine, N. and Macbeth, F. (1992) *Playing with Fire*. Leicester: Youth Work Press.

Freire, P. (1982) *Pedagogy of the Oppressed*. Harmondsworth: Penguin.

Fullan, M. (1991) *The New Meaning of Educational Change*. London: Cassell.

Glasser, W. (1998) *Choice Theory*. New York: HarperCollins.

Goldson, B. (2000) *The New Youth Justice*. Lyme Regis: Russell House.

Goleman, D. (1996) *Emotional Intelligence*. London: Bloomsbury.

Graef, R. (2000) *Why Restorative Justice?* London: Calouste Gulbenkian Foundation.

Griffiths, M. (2003) *Returning the Favour – Sharing CRISP Learning Experiences*. Leicester: CRISP, Leicester Mediation.

Hargreaves, A. and Fullan, M. (1998) *What's Worth Fighting For in Education?* Maidenhead: Open University Press.

Hayes, H., Prenzler, T. and Wortley, R. (1998) *Making Amends: Final Evaluation of the Queensland Community Conferencing Pilot*. Queensland: Griffith University.

Holdaway, S., Davidson, N., Dignan, J., Hammersley, R., Hine, J. and Marsh, P. (2001) *New Strategies to Address Youth Offending: The National Evaluation of the Pilot Youth Offending Teams*. RDS Occasional Paper No. 69. London: Home Office.

Holt, J. (1966) *How Children Fail*. London: Pitman.

Holton, L. (2002). Personal communication.

Jackson, S. (1998) *Family Justice? An Evaluation of the Hampshire Youth Justice Family Group Conferencing Project.* Southampton: University of Southampton.

Johnston, G. (2002) *Restorative Justice – Ideas, Values, Debates.* Cullompton, Devon: Willan Publishing.

Kingston Friends Workshop Group (1996) *Ways and Means Today.* Kingston upon Thames: Kingston Friends Workshop Group.

Kohn, A. (1999) *Punished by Rewards.* New York: Houghton Mifflin.

Lakoff, G. and Johnson, M. (1980) *Metaphors We Live By.* Chicago and London: University of Chicago Press.

Lampen, J. and Lampen, D. (1997) *What If's in Peer Mediation.* Stourbridge: The Hope Project.

Levine, M., Eagle, A., Tuiavi'L, S. and Roseveare, C. (undated) *Creative Youth Justice Practice.* Wellington: Social Policy Agency, and Children, Young Persons and Their Families Service.

MacGilchrist, B., Myers, K. and Reed, J. (1997) *The Intelligent School.* London: Paul Chapman Publishing.

McCold, P. (2002) *Evaluation of a Restorative Milieu: CSF Buxmont School/Day Treatment Programs 1999–2001.* International Institute for Restorative Practices. Retrieved in December 2002 from www.iirp.org

McNeely, C.A., Nonnemaker, J.M. and Blum, R.W. (2002) 'Promoting School Connectedness: Evidence from the National Longitudinal Study of Adolescent Health.' *Journal of School Health 72,* 138–146.

Mapp, S. (1997) 'Family Group Therapy'. *Community Care,* 8–14 May.

Margetts, D. (2002) Personal Communication.

Marsh, P. and Crow, G. (1998) *Family Group Conferences in Child Welfare.* Oxford: Blackwell Science.

Marshall, T. and Merry, S. (1990) *Crime & Accountability.* London: Home Office.

Maxwell, G. and Morris, A. (1993) *Family, Victims and Culture: Youth Justice in New Zealand.* Wellington: Social Policy Agency, and Institute of Criminology, Victoria University of Wellington.

Mediation UK (2001) *The Rough Guide to Restorative Justice & the Crime and Disorder Act.* Bristol: Mediation UK.

Miers, D., Maguire, M., Goldie, S., Sharpe, K., Hale, C., Netten, A., Uglow, S., Doolin, K., Hallam, A., Enterkin, J. and Newburn, T. (2001) *An Exploratory Evaluation of Restorative Justice Schemes.* London: Home Office.

Mirsky, L. (2002) *A New Reality for Troubled Youth in Hungary: An Update.* International Institute for Restorative Practices. Retrieved in December 2002 from www.iirp.org

Moore, D. and Forsythe, L. (1995) *A New Approach to Juvenile Justice: An Evaluation of Family Conferencing in Wagga Wagga.* New South Wales: Charles Sturt University.

Morris, K. and Tunnard, J. (eds) (1996) *Family Group Conferences – Messages from UK Practice and Research.* London: Family Rights Group.

Morrison, B. (2002) 'Bullying and Victimisation.' *Trends and Issues in Crime and Criminal Justice 219,* 1–6.

Mosley, J. (1993) *Turn Your School Round.* Wisbech: LDA.

Mosley, J. and Tew, M. (1999) *Quality Circle Time in the Secondary School.* London: David Fulton Publishers.

Newburn, T., Earle, R., Goldie, S., Campbell, A., Masters, G., Crawford, A., Sharpe, K., Hale, C., Saunders, R. and Uglow, S. (2001) *The Introduction of Referral Orders into the Youth Justice System. Second Interim Report.* RDS Occasional Paper No. 73. London: Home Office.

Newburn, T., Earle, R., Goldie, S., Masters, G., Crawford, A., Sharpe, K., Hale, C., Netton, A., Saunders, R. and Uglow, S. (2002) *The Introduction of Referral Orders into the Youth Justice System. Final Report.* London: Home Office.

Peachey, D. (1989) 'The Kitchener Experiment.' In M. Wright and B. Galaway (eds) *Mediation and Criminal Justice.* London: SAGE.

Postman, N. and Weingartner, L. (1971) *Teaching as a Subversive Activity.* London: Penguin.

Preston, N. (2002) *Restorative Justice – A New School of Thought.* Chilton, Bucks: Thames Valley Partnership.

QCA/DfEE (1998) *Education for Citizenship and the Teaching of Democracy in Schools.* London: QCA/DfEE.

Reimer, E. (1971) *School is Dead.* London: Penguin.

Rosenberg, M. (1999) *Nonviolent Communication: A Language of Compassion.* Del Mar, CA: PuddleDancer Press.

Stone, D., Patton, B. and Heen, S. (1999) *Difficult Conversations.* New York: Michael Joseph.

Strang, H. (2000) *Victim Participation in a Restorative Justice Process: The Canberra Reintegrative Shaming Experiments.* PhD thesis. Centre for Restorative Justice, Australian National University.

Thames Valley Police (2001) *Restorative Interventions – Facilitator Skills Training.* Kidlington, Oxon: Thames Valley Police Restorative Justice Training Consultancy.

Thorsborne, M. (2003) Personal communication.

Tyrrell, J. (2002) *Peer Mediation: A Process for Primary Schools.* London: Souvenir Press.

Umbreit, M. (2001) *The Handbook of Victim Offender Mediation: An Essential Guide to Practice.* San Francisco: Jossey-Bass.

Umbreit, M. (2002) *Victims of Severe Violence Meet Offenders: Restorative Justice Through Dialogue.* Monsey, NY: Criminal Justice Press.

Umbreit, M. and Roberts A., (1996) *Mediation of Criminal Conflict in England: An Assessment of Services in Coventry and Leeds.* Saint Paul, MN: Center for Restorative Justice and Peacemaking, University of Minnesota.

Wright, M. (1996) *Justice for Victims and Offenders (Second Edition). Winchester: Waterside Press.*

Wright, M. (1999) *Restoring Respect for Justice.* Winchester: Waterside Press.

Yantzi, M. (1998) *Sexual Offending and Restoration.* Kitchener, Ontario: Herald Press.

Zehr, H. (1995) *Changing Lenses.* Scottdale, PA: Herald Press.

Zehr, H. (2002) *The Little Book of Restorative Justice.* Intercourse, PA: Good Books.

Zehr, H. and Mika, H. (1998) 'Fundamental Principles of Restorative Justice.' *The Contemporary Justice Review 1*, 47–55.

Useful Contacts

Restorative Justice in schools

My own organisation, which offers all the skills and approaches described in this book:

Belinda Hopkins
Transforming Conflict
Centre for Restorative Justice in Education
Mortimer Hill
Mortimer
Berkshire
RG7 3WP
Tel: 0118 9331520
E-mail: belinda@transformingconflict.org
Website: www.transformingconflict.org

People to contact who are also offering training in the UK:

Caroline Belmont
Sussex Centre for Restorative Justice
E-mail: info@sx-ctre-restjust.demon.co.uk

LEAP – Confronting Conflict offer many inspiring courses for those working with young people in challenging situations.
Tel: 020 7272 5630
E-mail: sue@leaplinx.com

Margaret Thorsborn and Associates
4 Kimbarra Court
Buderim 4556
Australia
Tel: +61 7 5445 3520
Fax: +61 7 5445 2857
Website: www.thorsborne.com.au
ABN: 70 083 072 486

Despite her Australian base, Margaret regularly comes to the UK to offer training.

Real Justice and the Restorative Training Practices Association (a partnership of Real Justice and Thames Valley Police) offer training in restorative interventions and approaches:

Nicola Preston
Training Co-ordinator
Restorative Practices Training Association
PO Box 2013
Buckingham
MK18 4YD
Tel: 01280 847437
Fax: 0709 211 1316

The Restorative Justice Consortium supports work in schools and has developed some national practice standards for this work. These and useful explanatory literature can be obtained from their website: www.restorativejustice.org.uk

Circle Time

Useful organisations to contact include:

Jenny Mosley
Jenny Mosley Consultancies
28a Gloucester Road
Trowbridge
Wiltshire
BA14 0AA
Tel: 01225 767157
Fax: 01225 755631
E-mail: circletime@jennymosely.demon.co.uk
Website: www.jennymosley.demon.co.uk

Lucky Duck Publishing Ltd.
3 Thorndale Mews
Clifton
Bristol
BS8 2HX
Tel: 0117 973 2881
Fax: 0117 973 1707
E-mail: Publishing@luckyduck.co.uk
Website: www.luckyduck.co.uk

Communication and Conflict Management

Center for Nonviolent Communication
2428 Foothill Boulevard
Suite E
La Crescenta
CA 91214 USA
Tel: +1 818 957 9393
E-mail: cnvc@cnvc.org

The website for the Center for Nonviolent Communication, founded by Marshall Rosenberg, carries information about Nonviolent Communication and a list of trainers worldwide: www.cnvc.org

Training in Nonviolent Communication is available from **Gina Lawrie** and **Bridget Belgrave**, whose website is www.liferesources.org.uk

Mediation (including peer mediation)

For current information about training in mediation and peer mediation contact:

Mediation UK
Alexander House
Telephone Avenue
Bristol
BS1 4BS
Tel: 0117 904 6661
E-mail: enquiry@mediationuk.org.uk
Website: www.mediationuk.org.uk

There is a **Young Mediators' Network** supporting secondary school mediators. Contact LEAP for more information (as above).

Family group conferencing

For training in this area contact:

Liz Holton
Family Group Conference and Schools Counselling Service Manager
County Education Office
The Castle
Winchester
Hants
SO23 8UG
Tel: 01962 846365
Fax: 01962 846469
E-mail: liz.holton@hants.gov.uk

Liz Holton runs family group conferences in schools around Hampshire. She also trains others to co-ordinate this process.

Simon Evans
RJ Solutions
E-mail: RJSOLUTIONS@aol.com
Website: www.rjsolutionsuk.org.uk

Resources

Excellent resources for developing restorative skills can be obtained from

Lucky Duck Publishing (see above) and from

Incentive Plus. Website: www.Incentiveplus.co.uk

Subject Index

Author Index